Leading Personalized and Digital Learning

Leading Personalized and Digital Learning

A Framework for Implementing School Change

Mary Ann Wolf
Elizabeth Bobst
Nancy Mangum

HARVARD EDUCATION PRESS
CAMBRIDGE, MASSACHUSETTS

Paperback ISBN 978-1-68253-091-7
Library Edition ISBN 978-1-68253-092-4

Library of Congress Cataloging-in-Publication Data

Names: Wolf, Mary Ann, author. | Bobst, Elizabeth, author. | Mangum, Nancy, author.
Title: Leading personalized and digital learning : a framework for implementing school change / Mary Ann Wolf, Elizabeth Bobst, Nancy Mangum.
Description: Cambridge, Massachusetts : Harvard Education Press, [2017] | Includes bibliographical references and index.
Identifiers: LCCN 2017019880| ISBN 9781682530917 (pbk.) | ISBN 9781682530924 (library edition)
Subjects: LCSH: Classroom environment—United States. | Group work in education—United States. | Team learning approach in education—United States. | Educational technology—United States. | Effective teaching—United States. | Motivation in education—United States.
Classification: LCC LB1032 .W655 2017 | DDC 371.102/4—dc23
LC record available at https://lccn.loc.gov/2017019880

Published by Harvard Education Press,
an imprint of the Harvard Education Publishing Group

Harvard Education Press
8 Story Street
Cambridge, MA 02138

Figure I.2 Design: Catherine Immanuel
Figure I.2 Images: iStock.com/appleuzr/-VICTOR-/Abert84
Cover Design: Wilcox Design
Cover Image: iStock.com/aleksandarvelasevic

The typefaces used in this book are Janson Text and Gotham.

Contents

Preface

Schools in the United States have endured many fads and phases, often embracing and discarding philosophies and approaches in search of the next best thing. Phonics or whole language? New math or old math? Common Core or traditional algebra? Again and again, school districts and politicians have adopted education approaches touted to find the one best and right way to reach every student. But seasoned educators know this search for the one right and true thing to be futile. There is no best way, no right way, no one way to engage every student in learning. Administrators and classroom teachers all have different backgrounds and bring distinct skill sets to their work each day. Teachers have varying depths of knowledge of their subjects as well as levels of curiosity. Each teacher has strengths and weaknesses. Every teacher is unique. Students also have individual learning strengths and differences. They bring their own interests and passions to school, as well as the effects of their personal living situations and families. Every student is unique.

Each of us vividly remembers a point when it became clear that the promise of high-quality education for all would not be realized without personalized learning.

Mary Ann Wolf remembers:

> Like many teachers, when I was teaching in a fifth-grade classroom nearly twenty years ago, I had students working on seven or eight different grade levels. One student, in particular, stands out at shaping my work in education for the twenty years since then. Riley came to me barely able to read. He could not even consistently read the high-frequency first-grade words. I quickly discovered, however, that Riley could remember the facts from our science or social studies lessons with ease. He listened, participated in activities, and could remember and apply complex ideas on the assessments if the questions were read aloud to him. I realized that Riley could learn, but the phonics and other traditional approaches that our school had been trying for five years had not worked for him.

I asked Riley if I gave him ten flashcards each day on a big ring if he would practice those words ten times each night. Each day we added ten more cards, and each night he would practice the new words and all of the words that he had received previously ten times. If I forgot to give him new cards, he always reminded me. Before long, Riley had eight hundred to one thousand words that he was practicing and reading. One of my very best moments of teaching happened when my students were reading a social studies passage in pairs. Riley's buddy John raised his hand and said, "Ms. Wolf, Riley won't let me read!" Riley had put together those hundreds of words and was now able to read almost any text.

While I was able to help Riley learn to read through personalized instruction and involving Riley in his own learning, I struggled with the fact that I could only truly personalize learning for a couple of students every day, despite my best efforts. I knew that each student could benefit from personalized learning, but there was no realistic way of bringing it about in my classroom.

Elizabeth Bobst remembers:

On the first day of my first year of teaching, I was introduced to Nathan by another seventh-grade student in the class. "This is Nathan. He's already been expelled from school—twice!" Nathan sat right in front of my desk and talked to me constantly. It didn't take long to figure out that Nathan was smart—likely brilliant. He loved ideas, the bigger the better. Instead of grammar rules, Nathan wanted to talk about apartheid. He had no interest whatsoever in the young adult coming-of-age novel I was teaching. He finished the novel in a day, summed it up (sardonically) in a few sentences, and was ready to move on. The rest of the class, however, had thirty more chapters and many discussions to get through.

By accident, I found something challenging for him to do. Someone in the class suggested making a movie of the novel we were reading. Nathan volunteered to write the script. As the screenwriter, he often spent time in the library working on the script. Nathan shared his writing project and the class goal of making a film with the librarian, and the librarian volunteered to teach Nathan how to storyboard, how to use a video camera, and how to edit film. Nathan, with the help of others in the class, chose filming locations around the school, cast parts in the film, and spent a week making a movie. A few weeks of postproduction work finished the film, which garnered rave reviews when we showed it at the all-school assembly.

Nathan became a leader during the creation of that film, engaged in learning new skills, and took a lot of pride in the final product. Because of this engagement and the independence it offered him, Nathan excelled in my class.

In other classes, he remained disengaged and acted out. Near the end of the school year, facing yet another expulsion for chronic bad behavior, Nathan withdrew from the school and enrolled in an experimental boarding school.

And Nancy Mangum remembers:

During my third year of teaching, I moved to a new school. The school structure was set up differently from many traditional schools, with open classrooms where three teachers shared responsibility for a classroom of fifty-five to sixty students. To create a positive learning environment, all three teachers needed to collaborate to deliver instruction and facilitate learning, ensuring the needs of all of the students were met. We conferenced with each student individually at the beginning of every quarter and created personalized education plans. Data notebooks helped students and teachers track progress and allowed students to play an integral role in monitoring their progress. These data notebooks allowed the students to set goals for themselves. Even my kindergarten students did this, and the responsibility and goal setting that it taught them were amazing to see, as they were able to talk with confidence about themselves as learners! The teachers met weekly with the curriculum coach to discuss the progress each child was making. We spent extra time talking about those students who were struggling, making plans for how we might better meet their needs. While we didn't have a lot of technology to help us with this tracking and the data notebooks were literally an individual binder each student kept on a shelf, we worked hard to personalize education for all the children by meeting them where they were and helping them set goals for themselves. The three years that I taught at this school helped shape my beliefs and understanding about what a personalized education could be and how, especially in a public school setting with a diverse student population, it was possible for us to create a learning environment that could meet the needs of all learners.

It became clear to us, through our experiences in the classroom, that education needed to embrace personalized learning. For students to fully engage in their own learning, all students must be involved in creating their own learning paths, and all of them must be supported in following those paths, making adjustments along the way. In the past, this degree of personalization in a classroom was not possible. Too many students, too few teachers, and too few resources did not allow for personalization at scale in a traditional school setting. Educators became accustomed to making compromises concerning student learning. Sometimes the students at the top were sacrificed; at other times, the students at the bottom. Often, the students in the middle skated by unnoticed. Because instruction couldn't be tailored to meet the needs of each individual student, failure of some sort was inevitable.

Now, however, advances in digital technology have created the opportunity for broad changes in the educational system. It is increasingly possible to meet all students where they are in their learning journey and to collaborate with each student to create an individual educational path to follow. Digital tools allow students to learn in a multitude of different ways from a seemingly infinite array of resources. Technology has progressed to the point that educators, students, and parents now have the capability to completely reshape the structure of classrooms and schools. The shift to utilizing personalized and digital learning in our classrooms is so much more than simply adding technology to an existing curriculum. Technology allows us to change the way schools define and enable learning and it provides us with the tools to make learning more relevant, immediate, and global.

Personalized learning that utilizes digital tools engages both students and teachers and transforms almost everything that happens in a traditional school. Shifting to personalized and digital learning is the next essential step in the evolution of teaching and learning in the United States and around the world. Personalized learning empowers students, engages them, and makes connections with and between students, meeting students where they are on their individual educational paths and traveling with them on their learning journeys. Educators no longer have to make do with failing students. We now have the ability to connect with every student.

Every school and every school leader's journey is also unique. There is no one right way to personalize and digitalize learning for schools. The field is still nascent but perhaps because so many educators see the need and the common sense of this approach, the interest is overwhelming. One thing, though, is crystal clear to us: as in so many change efforts, leadership is key. Making this fundamental shift has many pitfalls. Through our over seventy years of collective experience in education, we have worked with hundreds of district and school leaders who are making the transition to personalized and digital learning, and we have learned so much through our time in schools and their journeys.

Through our work at The Friday Institute, we have had the opportunity to create research-based programs that help these leaders transition to personalized and digital learning. We have implemented year-long cohort-based programs, helped facilitators in sixteen states lead school leaders through our programs, applied design thinking for school leaders to address their own challenges, and reached all fifty states and even eighty countries across the world through the Massive Open Online Course for educators (MOOC-Eds) on leading personalized and digital learning, coaching digital learning, and learning differences. We have written about personalized learning, the culture shift needed in schools, and leadership.

We have listened to the stories of school leaders, asked them critical questions, and helped them develop action plans to guide them toward their goals. All this work has led us to the conclusion that essential lessons exist for all principals, aspiring principals, and others who want to successfully implement personalized learning. Without heeding these essential lessons, efforts to personalize will flounder. We have identified eight lessons—we call them Leadership Essentials—and present a framework to introduce them to leaders in this book.

We can't tell you what approach is going to be successful in your classroom(s) or your school(s) because there is no one-size-fits-all plan. We can, however, give you a framework to use as a touchstone on your journey to create change in your schools. We also can give you examples of others who have made successful and significant changes in their educational environments, highlighting the strategies they used. Because we believe in distributed leadership, you will hear their voices in this book. We wrote this book to share what we have learned with school and district leaders who are in the middle of, just beginning, or even reflecting on implementation and determining next steps. We hope that you will dive into our book seeking to learn from others, while also creating your own personalized approach for your school.

Before we begin, we want to emphasize the three things we know to be true about school leaders:

1. They got their start in education because they want to help kids learn and reach their potential.
2. They are always trying to figure out how to improve teaching and learning to improve or strengthen student outcomes.
3. They work really, really hard.

In this book, we want to help you think about your role and consider how you can channel your hard work and ideas to maximize the potential for personalized and digital learning for your students. We want to build on your strengths and the great work you are already doing by sharing our insight from working with hundreds of school and district leaders across the country and world. At the same time, we also want to share with you specific examples of how some principals have approached this transition to personalized and digital learning. We are excited to dive in with you, and we look forward to continuing to exchange ideas through social media and invite you to join in our conversation at #LeadingPDL.

Introduction

Every child begins life curious and eager to learn. As James Zull says, learning "is just what the brain does."[1] Young children are energized by learning and have a seemingly endless desire to ask the questions they design so that they can learn about and make sense of the world around them. Being hardwired for learning coupled with being nurtured by their parents can set students up for success as they enter school. Nearly all children go to school excited to learn, believing they are smart and capable of learning.

As educators, we know that somewhere along their journey in our education system, we fail to engage many of our students, and we lose them. Sometimes we lose them physically when they drop out and disappear. More often, we lose them emotionally and intellectually when they stop paying attention or begin to believe their efforts don't matter. Many classrooms are populated with students who seem unmotivated or disengaged. According to the Right Question Institute, children begin asking questions around the age of two, and they reach their questioning peak at age four. Each year after that, students ask fewer and fewer questions.[2] Traditional schools—based on a factory model created at the turn of the twentieth century—often discourage curiosity and questioning; they tend to encourage students to be passive and compliant. Many students become adept at parroting back information they have learned because that is the primary skill they need to be successful, to get good grades, to be at the top of the class. Students rarely integrate knowledge or content into their own understanding of the world, nor are they encouraged to do so in the classroom. We teach students that what we value in schools is success, not failure. As educators, we have become accustomed to student failure, and we justify that failure as a necessary evil of our education system, a system that overvalues testing and performance and often loses sight of actual learning. Too often, we find ourselves trying to help students succeed in a system in which we don't fully believe.

Educators trying to meet the needs of each student realize the importance of stepping away from the traditional education system and its shortcomings and moving toward personalized learning. Businesses and corporations, students' future employers, also realize the need to move beyond an education system focused on compliance and conformity and toward a system in which students are actively engaged in their own learning. Collaboration and the ability to listen are prized skills in the workplace. Employers seek out people who can take initiative, think critically, and follow tasks through to completion. As *New York Times* columnist Tom Friedman wrote summarizing the results of the 2013 Program for International Student Assessment (PISA), "the most successful students are those who feel real 'ownership' of their education. In all the best performing school systems . . . 'students feel they personally can make a difference in their own outcomes and that education will make a difference for their future.'"[3] Personalized learning provides an avenue to increase agency among all learners in our schools and ensures that instruction meets the needs of each student.

Knowing that the education system must change if we want students to ultimately be prepared for and successful in our economy is both an opportunity and a responsibility for education leaders. This book is designed to support school and district leaders who know that educators must do more than re-create schools that approach learning as one-size-fits-all or learning based solely on summative assessments. This book is for leaders who want to build schools that personalize learning to meet the needs of each student, who want to keep students engaged and excited about learning itself, and who strive to change the experience for teachers and students in their schools immediately.

Personalized learning is not a new idea. As we dig into what personalized learning means, however, you will see that we are at a point where we can realize the potential of personalized learning at scale due to the influx of digital resources and tools, deeper understanding of how the brain works, connectedness to resources all over the globe, and access to data and systems that support teachers in meeting the needs of students in real time each day.

While many educators are ready to dive into personalized and digital learning, we also live with the realities of a large and complex education system. Changing an entrenched system can be difficult. Creating change takes energy and attention and a willingness to fail and begin again. Initiating change means opening the doors to your offices, your classrooms, your schools, and inviting people to join in the process with you. Launching into this work in your schools can be daunting and, at many times, overwhelming. But just as our students come to us ready to learn, we believe all of our educators come to work ready to help students learn and be successful. We have the opportunity to work with district and school leaders every day at the Friday Institute at North Carolina State University, and we are constantly reminded that people who choose to dedicate their lives to education care about students and learning. Sometimes in the mix of assessments, schedules, bad press, and demanding parents, we forget that educators enter this profession because they have a deep desire to help students reach their individual potential.

Teachers in schools who are effectively implementing personalized and digital learning tell us again and again that the first year of the transition to personalized learning makes them feel like a first-year teacher all over again. The transition can destabilize even the most seasoned teacher, and teachers, as well as their leaders, need to be prepared for that possibility. Teachers who have implemented changes toward personalized and digital learning in their schools also *all* add, "I could never go back." Personalized and digital learning empowers both students *and* teachers.

School leaders like you play *the* critical role in creating the environment for change, in creating schools and school cultures where administrators can tap into the commitment and understanding of teachers and the desire of students to learn and succeed. You are not alone in carrying out this change, but you have the opportunity—and the responsibility—to lead the way by building ownership among all stakeholders and providing a culture in your schools and classrooms that allows teachers and students to try new things, fail sometimes, and learn how to personalize effectively.

WHAT IS PERSONALIZED AND DIGITAL LEARNING?

In this book, and in our work, we adhere to the definition of personalized learning developed for the National Educational Technology Plan:

> Personalized learning refers to instruction in which the pace of learning and the instructional approach are optimized for the needs of each learner. Learning objectives, instructional approaches, and instructional content (and its sequencing) may all vary based on learner needs. In addition, learning activities are meaningful and relevant to learners, driven by their interests, and often self-initiated.[4]

We are not simply talking about creating reading groups based on Lexile levels or allowing students to choose their own topic for a prescribed project. Personalized learning is complex because it encompasses using a number of inputs (multiple data points about students beyond academic test scores), creating multiple opportunities for learning, addressing social and emotional learning, and helping students reflect on their own learning (metacognition).

When we look closely at personalized learning, we begin by examining the role of the teacher. It is important to understand and remember that personalized learning does not diminish the role of the teacher in the classroom or turn the teacher into a bystander. Personalized learning moves away from a teacher-directed classroom and toward a student-centered, collaborative classroom where teachers remain active and engaged in the learning process. Making this change seems simple enough, but in practice, it's tremendously difficult. Teachers have been taught to control their classrooms, control their students' behavior, and control the pace of learning. Teachers are rewarded for this control. To shift away from lock-step learning means that each stakeholder—educators, students, parents—has enough trust to let go of the control and enough understanding of personalization to be certain that what ensues will not be chaos and anarchy.

In reality, instead of chaos, the Four Cs of collaboration, critical thinking, communication, and creativity can take center stage, supported by effective instructional strategies designed to scaffold student learning. Personalized learning is not accidental and chaotic, and it is not putting each student in front of a computer to work independently. It is thoughtfully planned, carefully articulated, and consistently measured. It challenges educators and students to truly understand their strengths, needs, and differences. Personalized learning challenges all stakeholders to be involved, committed, and passionate about what they're doing each and every day.

HOW DO DIGITAL RESOURCES AND TOOLS
RELATE TO PERSONALIZED LEARNING?

Teachers have long understood the value of personalized learning for reaching and engaging every student, but in the past, few educators were able to implement personalized learning in schools in effective ways for all students every day. Digital learning is *the* game-changer in making personalized learning a reality. In the past decade, major progress in the development of digital content, tools, data dashboards, and gamification has dramatically changed what is possible in personalizing education. Digital content has become available in a multitude of different formats, encompassing varied learning approaches. Instead of asking students to continually try to learn material in the same way again and again when they do not understand, teachers now have the ability to provide several different strategies, resources, activities, and practices that meet learning differences, draw upon students' strengths, and address students' interests. Not all students have to be working on the same material at the same pace because of the myriad options digital resources offer both students and teachers. Personalized learning at scale must include digital learning.

Keeping up with and incorporating the latest technologies in their work can be intimidating for many teachers. Technology changes quickly, and it sometimes feels impossible to stay current, much less ahead of the curve. Students and other teachers can be important resources for educators when learning new technologies. In a personalized classroom, the teachers don't need to be "the experts." Students can learn from a variety of sources, *just as teachers can.* Teachers can learn about new technologies most effectively by jumping in and integrating digital tools and resources slowly into their practice. In a personalized classroom, students and teachers often learn together. According to Sarah Brown Wessling, 2010 National Teacher of the Year, when it comes to personalized learning, "We model learning. I need to be the lead learner."[5]

Personalized and digital learning creates a different classroom dynamic, but it does not lessen the importance of the teacher. If anything, the implementation of personalized and digital learning allows teachers to spend more time using their pedagogical expertise. Learning should not solely depend on teacher-directed content delivered in one way for all. Rather, teachers can now have students engaged in different work and can spend more time facilitating learning in small groups, in one-on-one conferences, through project-based learning or student content creation.

WHAT DOES PERSONALIZED AND DIGITAL LEARNING LOOK LIKE IN ACTION?

The question of what personalized and digital learning looks like in action has more than one answer. That answer will look different depending on the school, the grade level, and the approach adopted by the teacher and the school or district. Figure I.1, developed as part of the work in creating the NC Digital Learning Plan in 2015, succinctly demonstrates critical differences between our traditional education system and one that is personalized and utilizes the opportunities presented through digital learning.[6]

In this book, we explore some examples of what personalized learning can look like in action by highlighting what innovative schools and districts around the country are doing to bring personalized learning to scale through a variety of methods and models, including blended learning, personal pathways, competency-based learning, and project-based learning.

HOW IS LEADERSHIP FOR PERSONALIZED AND DIGITAL LEARNING DIFFERENT FROM LEADERSHIP IN GENERAL?

Leadership is considered second only to classroom instruction as an influence on student learning.[7] So, too, leadership is critical for an effective transition to personalized and digital learning. A school leader leads by developing the culture of the school through a coherent shared vision, modeling the type of teaching and learning, and supporting both teachers and students. Moving to personalized and digital learning often means a significant change in how teaching and learning happen. Principals need to establish a school culture that encourages and supports teachers taking risks, a culture that eliminates the fear of making a mistake, so that educators can grow and improve their own instructional strategies and designs. Supporting teachers in this manner models the opportunity for students to also take risks in creating and exploring with their own learning.

In his book *The Principal: Three Keys to Maximizing Impact*, Michael Fullan discusses the idea of the principal as a change agent, systems player, and lead learner.[8] These roles are central to the transition to personalized and digital

Figure I.1 Comparison of traditional instructional and digital-age learning models

Traditional instructional model	Digital-age learning model
One-size-fits-all instruction and instructional resources.	**Personalized learning** and flexible resources optimized for each student.
Advancement based primarily on time spent in class.	Advancement based on demonstrated **mastery** of the content and **competency** in applying what has been learned.
Fixed places and times for learning within school buildings.	**Anywhere and anytime learning**, inside and outside of schools, 24/7, with most learning blending face-to-face and online activities.
Teacher-centered instruction, with teachers as expert disseminators of content to classes of students.	**Student-centered instruction**, combining large group, small group and individualized learning, with teachers serving as facilitators and coaches.
Printed, static text, often out-of-date, as the dominant content medium for educational resources.	**Digital content** providing interactive, flexible and easily updated educational resources.
End-of-course standardized assessments of learning, primarily for accountability.	**Assessments integrated into learning activities** to provide ongoing information about students' achievement that can be used to improve teaching and learning.
Academics addressed in isolation, with schooling separated from informal learning experiences outside of school.	Project-based and community-based learning activities **connecting to students' lives outside of school**.

Source: Used with permission from The Friday Institute for Educational Innovation.

learning. Often, educators and parents are entering unfamiliar territory with the use of technology as an integral part of teaching and learning. The ability to garner ownership among these and other stakeholders, guide and coach teachers while setting expectations, and communicate with parents will make or break change efforts in a school. Our experience validates the importance of these tenets of effective leadership. However, personalized and digital learning also demands that principals are able to achieve the following goals:

- *Model.* Although principals have always had the opportunity to model in some way, in making the transition from teacher-centered to student-centered learning, they need to model their own use of digital learning tools to personalize their work with individual teachers, in using data, and in building professional learning networks (PLNs) with others inside and outside the school community.

- *Adapt to the pace of change.* The pace of change in education has been slow. It is almost cliché to discuss how education and schools have looked the same for the past one hundred years or more. However, the near constant arrival of new technologies and digital learning has dramatically altered this situation, and the pace of change is now greatly accelerated. Schools need to change; it is no longer possible for them to remain stagnant. Principals moving toward personalized and digital learning must develop new strategies and be prepared for the sometimes fast and furious pace of change in a system designed to maintain the status quo.

- *Articulate a shared vision.* How can principals lead a vision for personalized and digital learning when rich examples are nascent themselves? Schools and districts that are making tremendous progress may not be nearby and may or may not match the context of your school. Principals must guide their stakeholders in thinking about what they want teaching and learning to be for their students and arrange for them to see, either in person or virtually, examples of their vision.

You can easily see, then, how personalized and digital learning is increasing expectations for school leaders. Because working with school leaders is our passion, we wrote this book to provide needed guidance for principals, aspiring principals, and others who are looking to put the power of technology to work for student-centered learning.

HOW DO WE DEVELOP A FRAMEWORK FOR LEADERS?

Based on our work teaching and coaching school leaders and their teams in making the transition to personalized and digital learning, we have identified eight essential lessons that we believe are critical for success:

1. Create a vision focused on teaching and learning.

2. Engage stakeholders as part of the team from the beginning, but don't stop there!
3. Employ change management and distributed leadership.
4. Build a culture of trust in which it is acceptable to fail.
5. Develop professional learning that is personalized and job-embedded.
6. Empower students with the Four Cs.
7. Create systems and structures that are sustainable and adaptable.
8. Build human capacity with teams.

Figure I.2 A framework for leading personalized and digital learning

We have developed a framework that incorporates these lessons for easy reference. As figure I.2 illustrates, a vision of personalized learning is the center of this effort. We go into each lesson in depth in the following chapters and summarize key actions for executing each.

This framework is not linear, but rather circular. Implementing personalized and digital learning is not a step-by-step process, but is iterative and cumulative. Notice that creating a vision is placed at the middle. This placement reflects our experience that without vision, and a commitment to promoting it and tying all efforts back to this vision periodically and at all phases, leaders will stumble in doing this work. Also notice that the word *technology* does not appear in this framework. This omission reflects our belief that when it comes to personalized learning, technology needs should be driven by the vision for teaching and learning and not the other way around. This transition is never about the technology itself, but about how we utilize technology to improve the data, assessments, curricula, and instruction.

In the same way that learning cannot be one-size fits-all, a leader and a school's approach to personalized and digital learning will look and roll out differently from school to school. Schools and districts will vary in how they approach or lead their personalized and digital learning efforts. These differences are part of the challenge and also the opportunity of talking about and implementing personalized education. We have included some specific and unique examples of schools that are leaders in personalized learning to help you imagine the scope of what is possible:

- *Summit Public Schools.* Starting in California and expanding to other states, Summit has moved aggressively toward personalized learning with an emphasis on using digital learning, data dashboards, and consistent feedback from students and teachers. These schools address content knowledge and cognitive skills specifically, as well as expeditions based upon interest and habits of success and use individual playlists (personalized digital assignment charts) for students. They also offer and utilize The Summit Learning Platform to facilitate personalized learning.
- *Teach to One.* Previously, the New Classrooms' model that originated as the *School of One* in New York City, *Teach to One* focuses on daily playlists for each student. These playlists are created based on where the students are on the learning standards, as well as the learning ap-

proaches and strategies that are most effective based on data that is gathered and student learning preferences.

- *Mooresville Graded School District.* Mooresville has been engaged in a digital conversion since 2007. While a device for each student is part of the implementation, Mooresville leaders are intentional about keeping the focus on personalizing teaching and learning, as well as the critical role of professional learning for teachers. Mooresville teachers use data, both academic and more holistic, to understand the needs of the students and to ensure that the curriculum and instruction supports the students in meeting their potential. Mooresville's graduation and achievement rates are among the highest in North Carolina, despite a higher-need population and lower cost per pupil expenditure.

- *Baltimore County Public Schools.* BCPS has been leading the charge with personalized and digital learning while always maintaining a focus on instruction and employing innovative digital content, even creating their own interactive textbooks to help prepare students for college science and other areas. BCPS utilized a pilot approach to transition to expanding personalized and digital learning across the large district based on interest and capacity of individual schools.

In addition, we have included insights from nine exemplary leaders who have helped shape our thinking. These leaders are representative of the talented and innovative educators we work with each day. They have taken the lead in personalizing learning in their schools, with demonstrable records of improving student outcomes. Indicative of their talents, several principals have been tapped for new positions since we interviewed them for this book. These leaders and their actions exemplify the Leadership Essentials we feature in this book. They are all dynamic and creative leaders who are deep thinkers. We believe that their ideas, strategies, and lessons learned will help you ask and answer critical questions and support you on your own journeys as you learn about and lead your own transitions into personalized and digital learning.

The principals who share their stories in this book represent schools with different grade levels, geographic locations, and demographics. Their schools include those in very rural areas of Alabama and North Carolina; more suburban schools in Iowa and Oregon; and urban schools in Charlotte, North Carolina, and Cleveland, Ohio. Some have higher socioeconomic status (SES), whereas some have very high free and reduced lunch populations. Their schools are primarily public schools, with representation from charter and private schools. These principals are energized and eager to share their stories with you. We invite you to connect with them and learn more about what they do.

- **Michael Armstrong** (Facebook: Michael Armstrong) is a first-generation college goer who became the principal of Bugg Creative Arts Magnet School in Raleigh, North Carolina, in 2011, an elementary school where 90 percent of students qualify for free or reduced lunch. In his three years at Bugg, Michael implemented a one-to-one personalized learning environment making use of iPads, personal electronic portfolios, and student-led conferences that resulted in greater student engagement, less absenteeism, and more involved parents. He is currently a doctoral student and working as a professional learning consultant.
- **John Bernia** (Twitter: @MrBernia) was the principal of Carleton Middle School in Sterling Heights, Michigan, a Title One school with a growing population of English language learners. John utilized creative approaches to professional learning to transform his school with personalized and digital learning. He was named a Digital Principal of the Year by the National Association of Secondary School Principals (NASSP) in 2015. He is currently the chief academic officer of Warren Consolidated Schools.
- **Erin Frew** (Twitter: @erin_frew) is the former principal of New Tech West High School in Cleveland, Ohio, where she implemented cross-curricular project-based learning with the support of one-to-one computing. With a focus on empowering students, she helped raise the school's performance index 9.9 points, taking her school from the "Continuous Improvement" category to "Effective" in one year. Erin was appointed to a district leadership position in the summer of 2016.
- **Alison Hramiec** (www.bacademy.org) is the head of Boston Day and Evening Academy in Roxbury, Massachusetts, a student-centered, competency-based charter school serving any Boston Public School student who has dropped out, is over-age, or is seeking a more flexible environment in which to earn a high school diploma. Alison led the redesign of the school's competency-based program, in which students

are placed in courses based on their academic needs, track their own learning, and move on after meeting agreed-upon benchmarks.

- **Suzanne Lacey** (Twitter: @TCBOE) is superintendent of Talladega County Schools in Alabama, a high-need, economically distressed district. Suzanne implemented a comprehensive approach to integrate digital learning through a districtwide focus on project-based learning, which offers students a choice in the way they learn and demonstrate mastery. All high schools are now in a one-to-one environment, but the focus remains on personalized learning and building capacity among her teachers and administrators. Under her leadership, the graduation rate increased from 68 percent in 2008 to 94 percent in 2015.

- **Tim Lauer** (Twitter: @timlauer) is the former principal of Meriwether Lewis Elementary School in Portland, Oregon, where he focused on finding the strengths among his teachers to build momentum and capacity while modeling personalized and digital learning. He challenged teachers to utilize their one-to-one environment in grades two through five (Chromebooks) to interact with students on and about their work and to use the dashboard to inform teaching and learning. Tim emphasized distributed leadership and using social media and other avenues to share the effective teaching and learning in his school among teachers and with parents and the community. He is currently a district leader in Washington state.

- **Derek McCoy** (Twitter: @mccoyderek) is the principal of West Rowan Middle School in Mount Ulla, North Carolina. He focuses heavily on student-centered learning, modeling the use of digital learning, and literacy across the curriculum. Derek addresses the importance of teacher mindset and learner agency head-on and strives to make spaces throughout the building and the digital environment collaborative. West Rowan is the second school that Derek has led through the transition to personalized and digital learning. Derek was named a Digital Principal of the Year by the NASSP in 2013.

- **Troy Moore** (Twitter: @MarinerscsK8) is the former principal of Hawk Ridge Elementary School in Charlotte, North Carolina, one of several Personalized Learning (PL) schools in the Charlotte-Mecklenburg schools. Troy launched personalized learning at Hawk Ridge by working directly with his teachers, and other stakeholders create personalized learning pathways. District results indicate students in the PL schools have shown greater growth in math and higher engagement. Currently, Troy heads the Mariners Christian School in Costa Mesa, California.

- **Amy Rickard** (Twitter: @MGESPrincipal) has been the principal of Morris Grove Elementary School in Chapel Hill, North Carolina, since it opened in 2007. Amy focuses heavily on creating culture based on collaboration and growth mindset, as well as the thoughtful integration of digital learning and cross-classroom opportunities to meet the needs of students.

HOW CAN THIS BOOK GUIDE YOU AND YOUR WORK?

As an education leader, you have the ability to bring personal and digital learning to your school and to create a seismic paradigm shift. You also have the ability to influence other educators and stakeholders to engage in this process with you. You understand that the time for this shift is *now*. Every day we wait, every year we make only incremental progress, means that another fifty-five million students are not getting the education that they truly deserve.

In each chapter of this book, you will find

- advice and examples in their own voices from principals who led the transition from traditional to personalized and digital learning
- research-based explanations
- a list of "Try It Tomorrow" activities that you can try with your teachers or stakeholders

Beginning or continuing this transition to personalized and digital learning and even choosing to read this book take courage. It is often easier to stay the course you and your school are currently on. If you are in a more traditional school or top-down district, it may be easier to follow the dictates of the district leaders. If you have solid test scores, it may be simpler to keep parents happy and allow students to keep going. You are choosing a challenging path, but you should know that resources are available to help support you. Visit our website, leadingpersonalizeddigitallearning.com, to discover more ways to connect with people doing this dynamic work. Change is difficult, but many principals, coaches, and teachers remind us that the benefits of personalized learning are well worth the struggle.

1

Create a Vision for Teaching and Learning

You don't start the talk with technology;
you start with pedagogy.

—DEREK MCCOY

You may fundamentally agree that shifting to personalized and digital learning is essential for all students to find success, but you may find yourself in a school setting where it is difficult to convince anyone to change what isn't broken. If standardized test scores are strong, parents, teachers, and other stakeholders question why anything needs to change. Yet students deserve and need more. Some schools that have many students identified as high need or at risk, however, may have pressure to focus on the basics or "drill and kill" to be prepared for the test. Every school situation is unique, and each requires an understanding of what students in that school need so that they are prepared for college, career, and citizenship. The idea that "knowledge is power" is true only to a certain point compared to fifty or even twenty years ago. Kristen Vogt reports, "Harvard professor Roland Barth has observed that in the 1950s when young people left high school they typically knew about 75% of what they would need to know to be successful in life. Today, he predicts that young people know about 2% of what they will need to know. . . ."[1]

The transition to personalized and digital learning should compel us to think about the purpose and focus of schools and learning and to understand that the purpose and focus are shifting and changing. Are schools about the adults or the students? While we know the answer, the way we create structures and even learning opportunities often focuses more on the role of the adults than the students.

EXAMINE FUNDAMENTAL BELIEFS
ABOUT TEACHING AND LEARNING

Educators begin teaching with a desire to help students succeed. As they prepare and lead lessons, teachers typically find that some students learn quickly, whereas others struggle to master the material or, worse, do not even seem to care about learning. Two master educators crafted questions to consider when diving into what personalized learning means for you and your school. Posing these questions to the teachers and parents in your school may help you begin to identify the vision for teaching and learning.

Kim Carter of QED asks this poignant question: "Which of the following statements do you believe: kids do well because they can OR kids do well because they want to?"[2] The first statement implies that educators ensure students have what they need to learn, even if that looks different for different students, whereas the other implies that students make a choice to learn or succeed. While most educators might argue that they believe the first, many of our classrooms operate in such a way that tends to suggest the latter. Are teachers focused on the learning or on a student's ability to check the boxes? Do teachers try to create multiple ways for students to learn material, especially if they are having trouble, without penalty? Do students have the opportunities to show what they have learned in a way that most meets their needs and strengths? Do we think we are giving students an unfair advantage by allowing them to try again and learn something in a different way?

Teachers must make a fundamental decision to assume responsibility for creating learning environments that meet the needs of each student. A teacher's mindset determines how she approaches not only instruction but also what beliefs she communicates to each student. When a school and teachers begin to implement personalized learning, educators must believe in the potential of every student and also believe that it is acceptable if some students need different opportunities and supports to learn.

John Bernia, former principal of Carleton Middle School, asked another set of questions to help teachers think differently about their instruction: "Did you teach it OR did the students learn it? These are very different ideas. Once you identify that, and focus on the fact that you want them to learn, some changes need to happen. It may be that students need to talk more, and you need to listen more. Students need to be able to ask more questions, or they need to demonstrate something to you. You may need to be more flexible—loosen the reins."

Personalized learning demands that students are able to ultimately be successful and learn. The question is how we get to a point where that can happen? It is the responsibility of the leaders and teachers to ensure that the environment and the instruction are available to maximize each student's potential. The culture of the school supports the idea that students will learn, even though the instructional strategies, the timing, and ultimately the supports needed will vary. Failure is not an option when everyone is committed to understanding how each student can learn effectively; and personalized learning provides a lens to push ourselves to better understand academic achievement, learning differences, and other aspects of each student.

CREATE A VISION WITH STAKEHOLDERS

While having a vision for teaching and learning sounds like an obvious imperative for a school or district, in many cases, a true, coherent vision is lacking. "Although they say it in different ways, researchers who have examined education leadership agree that effective principals are responsible for establishing a schoolwide vision of commitment to high standards and the success of all students."[3]

The failure to develop a vision focused on teaching and learning is often cited as the biggest pitfall in a personalized and digital learning effort. Although many principals have a vision, that vision might have been created in isolation without input from stakeholders or, even worse, created but never shared, creating confusion and making it difficult to gain momentum for change.

Engaging parents, students, community members, and teachers in this discussion is essential and a powerful way to create a shared vision and to quickly see that there is more agreement than disagreement in most groups. Starting the discussion with questions about a vision for digital learning, devices, or even new content can allow the schools to miss the reason that personalized and digital learning makes sense in the first place. The shift to personalized learning needs to start with pedagogy. Many different strategies can be used to create the vision, but the key is that it must begin with teaching and learning.

As you think about introducing the idea of a shared vision of teaching and learning or of focusing on personalized and digital learning, you may receive some negative reactions or frustration. How often do you hear teachers say in exasperation, "What do they want us to do now?" "I was just getting used to this curriculum or schedule," or "I wonder how long this will last?" Parents ask, "Why are my children learning this way?" They may even dig their heels in, saying, "We were taught the old-fashioned way and it worked fine. Why are you changing it now?"

This confusion or even exhaustion from jumping from initiative to initiative can complicate your job as you move forward in a transition to personalized and digital learning. Stakeholders are wary of change, and convincing them of the need for change can be difficult. Part of your work is to show, by example, that this way of learning is not something to be added on to the side or the top of other work. Personalized and digital learning is not another initiative or another thing to try this year. Instead, personalized and digital learning *is* the teaching and learning; it is the work of the teachers, students, administrators, and parents in your school.

One of the reasons that teachers, students, and parents feel as though something is always being added is that schools often bring in new initiatives or programs without taking anything away or explaining to stakeholders how the new initiative connects to existing programs. More often than not, *more* rarely means *better*. Once the vision for the school has been established, it is important to hold everything up to the light of that vision and ask, "Does this new initiative support our vision? Does this new program help us get where we want to go?" Alison Hramiec, head of Boston Day and Evening Academy (BDEA), advises, "Leaders must be willing to say no and sometimes accept that what we've just spent years working on doesn't really meet our needs in helping us to achieve our vision. There is no one-size-fits-all solution." Sometimes, institutional programs or projects have run their course and no longer serve the vision for the school. Teachers often look to the principal for permission to let a program go, and principals should listen and be prepared to support a "no" decision. If educators understand and trust that you are planning to stop a program or willing to say no to some requirements or initiatives, they will be more open to exploring the new vision for teaching and learning.

Classroom teachers are the closest to pedagogical practices, and they have the most expertise in instruction. They have a deep understanding of students and teaching and learning. However, teachers are often left out of the vision development process. They are rarely asked, "How do *you* think this should work?" Instead, teachers can feel that things are done *to* them. Respecting teachers' knowledge and experience by engaging them in the brainstorming, planning, and communication of the vision for the transition to personalized and digital learning boosts teacher buy-in and morale and also accelerates the implementation. Principal Troy Moore recently transitioned to Mariners Christian School from Hawk Ridge Elementary School. Troy had a tremendously positive and successful experience with personalized learning at Hawk Ridge, so when he was charged by Mariner's Christian to move the school toward personalized learning, he could have jumped into his new situation with that vision from his old school. Instead, he understood that this school was a new and unique context that included different teachers and students, as well as different parents and communities. Based on the expressed needs of stakeholders, Troy decided to focus early on literacy instruction in the transition to personalized learning. He said:

> At my new school, we needed to make a shift within the elementary literacy instruction. I am very pro Reading Workshop model within the Units of Study, based on the ideas of Lucy Calkins. I could have just said to the teachers and parents, this is what we are going to do; but instead, we had Socratic discussions on the state of the current literacy program. I bought units for the grade levels to try out, and I trained them on some areas myself and brought in some mid-level experts from Charlotte to further develop them. I had planned on continuing this way from October through May and then make a decision about where to go next. I had only asked them to try out some things. In December, the elementary teachers hijacked a staff meeting, said they all loved it, and wanted to formally adopt the curriculum at that point. There was true buy-in, and teachers felt respected and like true experts in the classroom. Upon the roll-out to parents, the teachers were the experts.

When we look across the schools and districts that have been most successful in creating a vision for personalized learning and implementing it, these schools have leaders who have been able to work with stakeholders from the beginning to build a cohesive vision that emphasizes that personalized and digital learning is essential to the vision and the work of the school itself. While this way of thinking sounds logical, it takes very purposeful decision making and conscious efforts to make it a reality. We will reference stakeholders frequently around creating a vision because working with them is a critical early step.

Many schools fall into the trap of adopting technology before understanding how they are going to use it or how it fits into their overall vision. Many schools or districts have been eager to move toward providing digital learning experiences and technology for their students. In an effort to have a one-to-one initiative (one device for every child), more technology-rich classrooms, or perhaps the devices for mandatory state online testing, schools and districts rush to implement technology without focusing first on a vision of what they want teaching and learning to look like in their schools. At the Friday Institute at North Carolina State University, we work with principals who often share that they have been implementing a one-to-one initiative for two or three years, but instruction has not really changed. This lack of change often means that the focus has been on the technology or the devices rather than on understanding student-centered, personalized learning. Personalized or digital learning initiatives that lead with the technology will *not* lead to improved outcomes for students. Change efforts must remain laser-focused on personalizing student learning, specifically by making learning more active and available anytime, anywhere. Digital learning certainly plays a critical role, but it must be considered in relation to how it supports a personalized approach for students. The development of the vision is critical to help leaders and teachers stay focused on learning and to avoid the pitfall of adding on or using digital learning as "one more thing" rather than seeing it as central to teaching and learning.

DECIDE WHAT YOU WANT TEACHING AND LEARNING TO LOOK LIKE IN YOUR SCHOOL

Where do you begin? Have you ever stopped and formally asked the teachers in your school what they want for your students? Similarly, have you asked students and parents? We often start visioning work with school leaders by asking, "What do you want teaching and learning to look like for your teachers and students in two to three years?" Three years is a reasonable interval to imagine, but the time frame is also actionable, implying that you will begin moving quickly. This question is a critical one for teachers, administrators, instructional coaches/media coordinators, parents, and students to consider.

It allows for the removal of trends or initiatives from the discussion and goes to the heart of why we are all in education.

Encourage your stakeholders to think freely and try to envision what schools might look like without the burden of what they have been in the past. Asking them to imagine what teachers and students would be doing if you walked into a classroom or what the furniture might look like helps stakeholders begin to describe the learning. One approach to getting input on teaching and learning is to provide stakeholders—whether teachers, students, parents, community members, or a cross-section of these groups—with the opportunity to collaborate through words, pictures, or other modes of expression. For example, school or district teams who come to the Friday Institute to better understand the transition to personalized and digital learning are asked to create a visual representation of what they want teaching and learning to look like. This approach often helps stakeholders avoid the trap of word-smithing and keeps them focused on what is important. Groups of teachers, parents, or district leaders should have the opportunity to develop and share their ideas collaboratively, participating in a learning process similar to one that might occur in a classroom. A faculty meeting can be an effective context for the school's staff, and a PTA or other community meeting can work for parents, students, and community members. Many common themes tend to emerge, and they are often creative and innovative. Ideas around collaborating, introducing self-paced learning, engaging students, fostering creativity, and ensuring relevant learning frequently come out in these discussions. Many groups also arrive at more project-based, student-centered learning.

Following are some examples from school and district leaders when asked for their vision:

- Students will have engaging and differentiated learning experiences led by creative, high-energy, effective teacher facilitators. Students will have access to high-quality, relevant, and rigorous resources that will support them in meeting the demands of a changing world.
- For students to discover through personalized learning and choice, digital leaders will have to reinvent themselves and remodel their instructional design. This will level the playing field, using technology as an accelerant for achievement.

- Learning should be facilitated by teachers who have embraced change to create both formal and informal instruction that meets all students' needs, allowing them to collaborate, communicate, create, and think critically. Technology is used to level the playing field for all students, deliver differentiated instruction to increase student engagement, enhance teaching and learning in the classroom, and is recognized as one of many tools or resources.

We have facilitated many cohorts at the Friday Institute and have used this visioning exercise numerous times. We've never had a single group say that they want all students learning the same thing at the same time in the same way in rows with a teacher at the front of the room. Even if stakeholders do not yet have the exact vision for what they want, they do begin to stretch their thinking and they do so collaboratively.

As district or school leaders go back and work with their stakeholders to develop the shared vision, they typically become more succinct and focused. Mooresville Graded School District developed a vision, mission, and motto:

- *Vision:* The vision of the Mooresville Graded School District is to ensure the maximum achievement of all students, resulting in a lighthouse district both nationally and internationally.
- *Mission:* The mission of the Mooresville Graded School District is to prepare every student, every day to be a successful and responsible citizen in a globalized workspace, economy and community.
- *Motto:* Every Child. Every Day.[4]

Talladega County Schools in Alabama developed a vision and a core purpose, which they share on their website:

- *Vision:* To provide an engaging, rigorous curriculum empowering all students to be college and career ready.
- *Core Purpose:* To ensure exemplary student performance, citizenship, and leadership.[5]

Interestingly, both Mooresville and Talladega share a set of beliefs that accompany their vision, and these beliefs serve almost as their philosophy of education. This effort can certainly support the culture and the embodiment of a shared vision.

Facilitating conversations about what learning might look like in the classroom can set the stage for the development of a shared vision. This vision may also encompass what the learning environment may look like, including classrooms, common space, and the library media center. While you, as the school leader, can certainly moderate the discussion, you may also want to consider asking someone outside the school (a trusted colleague, a university professor or other partner with strong facilitation skills) to assist so that you can participate along with your team. Whether you or a colleague facilitates the discussion, try to let the discussion unfold without jumping in to respond or to defend. Doing so often takes a conscious choice not to try to explain.

That vision then becomes the North Star for future decisions and the adoption of new strategies or the dropping of those programs that don't support the vision. Securing a shared vision provides a framework for future discussions of whether something supports a school's vision for teaching and learning. Many more decisions and ideas must be developed, planned, and implemented, but coming to consensus on what is the heart of teaching and learning provides great opportunities to make personalized and digital learning a reality.

IDENTIFY ESSENTIAL COMPONENTS OF PERSONALIZED AND DIGITAL LEARNING

One vision, one answer, or one model does not exist for personalized and digital learning. Personalized and digital learning efforts can come under many different names (such as blended learning, competency-based learning, digital conversion, social emotional learning, or project-based learning), and many of them may encompass some or many of the characteristics of personalized and digital learning. Summit Public Schools, Talladega County Schools, Baltimore County Schools, and Mooresville Public Schools each have different visions for personalized learning, utilizing different language and highlighting different areas of concentration.

When people describe to us what personalized learning looks like, they talk about something messier and even noisier than what we imagine in a more traditional classroom. Students and teachers might be doing different tasks and could be working on different content. Students may be collaborating with other students, working with a teacher, or working alone. Students may be determining what they do next, with guidance from a teacher, rather than relying on teachers to tell them what to do. More than one teacher may be working with a larger group of students, and the space may look more like a coffee shop than a traditional classroom. You will rarely see all students sitting quietly while a teacher delivers a lesson.

For many teachers and administrators, this kind of learning environment is hard to imagine. It can be uncomfortable to take the leap to see how this works in your school or classroom. Teachers often talk about feeling as though they're giving up their sense of control and handing it over to students. For teachers who are comfortable in a traditional role, this loss of control is a frightening prospect. When we delve deeply into culture and trust, you will quickly see that trusting students is as important as trusting the other adults in the building. Teachers and other stakeholders must believe that students can work independently and that they will check in as needed. All adults in the building must believe that if students care about and know why they are learning, their independent time on a device or on a project will be productive. When students know what to do and how to do it, and they have ownership over their own learning, rebalancing classroom control leads to increases in student engagement, focus, and learning.

This description of personalized and digital learning emphasizes its indefinite nature. While personalized learning can look different in every school and can even be different at different times in different classrooms in the same school, essential components or common themes arise that will help you in creating and ultimately implementing your vision. The following components of the vision for personalized and digital learning are meant to be guideposts as you develop your own vision with your stakeholders. Context matters. What your school community values will influence your vision, and the implementation of that vision will be unique. Fortunately, you can learn from the examples of other schools, and you will likely incorporate some similar essentials that other schools have included.

In our work, we have found these components to be essential:

- using standards to drive content
- allowing flexibility in pace
- moving from teacher-centered to learner-centered instruction
- developing learner agency

- utilizing the Four Cs
- recognizing digital learning as integral to personalized learning

Use Standards to Drive Content

Personalized and digital learning should be based on the standards set by the school, district, or the state. Not including standards in your vision or even in how you talk about personalized learning can leave you vulnerable for criticism or misunderstanding. Standards create a common language and a common set of expectations for each student. At the core of each lesson and instructional strategy are the standards, but you need to reiterate and state that point frequently. As teachers begin to build their units of study, they should begin with the standards and then create pathways that lay out the sequence of the content. You do not want to limit what students do and what they learn by the standards themselves. For some students, meeting the standards is the goal; and for others, meeting the standard is just a springboard to launch a new exploration.

Allow Flexibility in Pace

Another inherent characteristic of personalized learning is flexibility in pace. Students cannot all be expected to learn at the same time and pace. You and your teachers are likely aware of where your students are in their achievement. For some schools, addressing pace comes under a competency-based approach in which students each progress through the standards based on their readiness and abilities. For example, Hawk Ridge Elementary in Charlotte-Mecklenburg schools in North Carolina implemented a competency-based approach through personalized pathways. Students not only learn at their own pace but also have deep understanding of where they are and where they are going. They have different options along the pathways and understand why they might choose different content and activities. These third, fourth, and fifth graders collaborate, work in small groups with teachers, utilizing technology as appropriate, and independently complete tasks.[6]

New Classrooms, a nonprofit initially developed as the *School of One* in the New York City Department of Education, implements a competency-based approach for middle school students through the *Teach to One: Math* program.

In this approach, students have a playlist created each day based on where they are in their own learning. The playlists are different for each student and offer several different types of activities designed to help the students learn the specific standards of focus. These activities may be small group instruction, game-based learning, independent practice, or project-based learning, and the activities are determined by how the students learn most effectively. Examples of these schedules and activities can be found on the Teach to One website.[7] At any given time, most students in the room may be working on a different standard or a different activity related to a standard. Teachers play a critical role in the classroom instruction, but the decisions are student-centered in that they are based on how students learn most effectively.

Alison provides an in-depth look at competency-based learning in her school, Boston Day and Evening Academy:

> BDEA's competency-based assessment system is grounded in the principles that when student academic expectations are transparent for each course and advancement is based on student demonstration of those academic expectations, the ownership of learning is transferred from teacher to student.
>
> To do this well, before a student starts at BDEA, we identify their academic strengths and learning gaps. Students take a series of assessments that help teachers identify their academic skills and content knowledge. Based on these assessments (in each subject area), students are placed in courses that meet their academic needs. They are not placed in classes based on their grade level or age. This is incredibly helpful, to students and teachers. Students are engaged with the content and skill-building curriculum because it is material they do not know or skills they do not have.
>
> BDEA teachers have mapped for each class clear academic learning outcomes and assessments. When students begin a course, they are presented with a course syllabus that includes the academic competencies and benchmarks they will be expected to learn and demonstrate along with an ideal timeline by which they should complete the assessments. The teacher is then charged with creating engaging and relevant curriculum that allows students to experience and learn the new skills so that they can confidently demonstrate their new knowledge through assessments of varying types. Students monitor their own academic progress as they move through the class. If they fall behind, they know what is required to catch up. At the end of a trimester, if a student has not completed the course requirements (assessments), we do not say they failed the course; we say they have not yet finished the course. The student will continue the course the next term, beginning where they

left off instead of starting all over with the new class. Students understand that they cannot move forward to the next class until they demonstrate the required benchmarks for that course. These practices and schoolwide systems are essential in shifting the ownership of learning from the teacher to the student, putting the student at the center of the learning.

Understanding the importance of flexibility in pace does not necessarily equal a schoolwide competency-based model, but the elements of understanding where students are in their own learning, providing different ways for the students to progress, and then allowing students to move at the pace right for them are important aspects of personalized learning.

Move from Teacher-Centered Toward Student-Centered Approach

Teacher-centered classrooms rotate around teachers who act as the holders and disseminators of knowledge. Teachers have the ownership over the instruction, and in teacher-centered classrooms, the focus is on the teaching, not the learning. Teachers teach the material, but students don't always learn it. When you talk with teachers and schools with a primarily teacher-centered approach or if you look at their guidance about instruction, the language is often very much focused on the adults in the building rather than the students.

In a student-centered classroom, the locus of control shifts away from the teacher. This change is often evident in the design of the classroom. Desks do not all point toward the teacher; space is designed to be more collaborative. Students do not do the same thing at the same time every day. Standards are still the focus, but here, instructional strategies and content do not assume that every student learns the same way. Students can begin to understand how they learn most effectively. Teachers do not see one way as the right or best way, but rather understand that what is effective for one student may not work for another. If a student does not learn a module or standard in algebra the first time, that student is expected to go on to the next one without mastering the first. Even more importantly, students are not asked to do the same thing again, hoping for a different result. Learning is based on what the students need, and teachers (often with students as active participants) create the learning opportunities to ensure that students can succeed.

Student-centered learning provides opportunities and learning experiences that are not one-size-fits-all, but rather are tailored to the individual needs of a student. Learning experiences may vary by pace, instructional strategies, and support. It is nearly impossible to be truly student-centered without moving away from instruction that is based solely on academic achievement, multiple-choice assessments, or every student doing the same thing at the same time. The student-centered approach requires understanding the complex combinations of characteristics and strengths of a student. While it is important to have data about a student's academic achievement, teachers and other supports in the school must also know more about a student's interests, passions, and learning differences and also address a student's social emotional learning. According to Liz Glowa and Jim Goodell,

> Education that is student-centered has tremendous potential, and recent results are promising:
> - Decrease in drop-out rates
> - Increase in percentage of students accepted into college
> - Increase in growth in mathematics—grade level indicators and state assessments
> - Increase in growth in reading—grade level indicators and state assessments
> - Increase in student engagement
> - Decrease in student referrals
> - Increase in student agency.[8]

Social emotional learning (SEL) is often discussed as building relationships with students and among students. However, educators that are expert in this area are quick to point out that SEL does not stop at relationships. On its website, the Collaborative for Academic, Social, and Emotional Learning (CASEL) states that its framework for SEL includes self-awareness, self-management, responsible decision making, and social awareness in addition to relationship skills.[9] This tool encompasses helping students build social and life skills, which requires providing opportunities for them to learn and practice these skills, as well as teaching them. Sharing what they know, expressing their needs, and relating to one another are critically important skills that some students do not learn at home. Teachers must be aware of these skills and also model them every day. Classrooms that address SEL look and feel different, and this change cannot be accomplished through a once-a-week lesson on one critical area. SEL can lead to improvements in employability and in how students interact with others. A study by Columbia University found that SEL could even be measured in economic terms with the implementation of six SEL-related interventions:

There is a positive return on investments for all of these educational reforms on social and emotional learning. And the aggregate result also shows considerable benefits relative to costs, with an average benefit-cost ratio of about 11 to 1 among the six interventions. This means that, on average, for every dollar invested equally across the six SEL interventions, there is a return of eleven dollars, a substantial economic return. These findings are robust to the imposition of different assumptions on the sources and construction of benefits and costs, and a full accounting for benefits, as shown in the benefit maps, would provide an even larger return.[10]

Sometimes interventions or beliefs related to SEL may be the first to go when budget cuts happen or when teachers and leaders are worried about high-stakes testing. This is a short-sighted decision. A meta-analysis across more than two hundred studies shows that "[c]ompared to controls, SEL participants demonstrated significantly improved social and emotional skills, attitudes, behavior, and academic performance that reflected an 11-percentile-point gain in achievement."[11] This research and our understanding of what students need to learn should remind us that incorporating SEL is imperative in this shift.

Develop Learner Agency

Learner agency is relevant for *all* learners in the school—the adults and the students. Although it is sometimes referred to as *student agency*, we use the term *learner agency* here to ensure that we do not forget that the educators also need and deserve ownership in their learning. Tom Vander Ark defines agency as "the capacity and propensity to take purposeful initiative."[12]

While learner agency incorporates voice, choice, and engagement, simply allowing students to choose a book or an activity is not enough. Students must set goals and understand where they are trying to go and then be empowered to drive and have ownership of their own learning. Students who have learner agency are not passive, and they do not wait for a teacher to tell them what they should do next.

Agency can make a significant difference in student outcomes and persistence. "According to Farrington and colleagues (2012), 'When students believe they are likely to succeed in meeting academic demands in a classroom, they are much more likely to try hard and to persevere in completing academic tasks, even if they find the work challenging or do not experience immediate success' (p. 29)."[13]

Research by the Raikes Foundation includes some key ways to better understand the depth of learner agency. Teachers may address some of these aspects of learner agency in their classrooms, whereas others may strive to reach these only at the beginning of school, never revisiting them again. These statements could be a good starting point for discussion with teachers or may help them better understand learner agency:

1. *Growth mindsets:* "I can learn."
2. *Self-efficacy:* "I can do this."
3. *Relevance and purpose:* "This is important to me."
4. *Social belonging:* "I belong here."
5. *Goal setting and management:* "These are my goals, and I can reach them."
6. Metacognition: "I know myself and what I need to do."
7. Social capital: "I can get help when I need it."[14]

You can imagine examples in your school where students express evidence of agency as found in these statements. Erin Frew, former principal of New Tech West High School in Cleveland, Ohio, says:

> My vision is that teachers leverage their resources—textbooks, written materials, outside folks—to be able to provide an education for students where students build their own capacity to be agents for themselves. We focus on talking about and teaching students how to learn and find their own information. For me, it's really important that we have an education that not just ensures that kids are career and college ready, but also productive citizens so that they can make good choices when they vote and when they're out in the community. One of the things that we've worked hard on over the past one and a half years is having students know their own learning story. We've involved the kids in thinking about "Where was I when I came in, and what is my goal for the year? How am I going to grow? What are the things I'm going to do?" The tenth-grade geometry teacher has them do a learning log. "What have I learned this week? What have I done to contribute to my own learning? What could I have done differently? What can I do differently next week?"

She further explains that this focus on learner agency led to significant increases in the school's winter NWEA assessments, and she attributes much of this growth to the students knowing themselves and what they do now and what they need to do in the future.

Having a school culture that encourages and supports learner agency for all, including the ability to try new things and fail, is an essential condition for transitioning to personalized learning. This theme of trying and failing should be present and emphasized in your vision for teaching and learning.

Utilize the Four Cs

The Partnership for 21st Century Skills and EdLeader 21 define the Four Cs as collaboration, critical thinking, communication, and creativity.[15] They are sometimes called twenty-first century skills. They are also closely related to another body of work called deeper learning. The Hewlett Foundation defines deeper learning as "a set of six interrelated competencies: mastering rigorous academic content, learning how to think critically and solve problems, working collaboratively, communicating effectively, directing one's own learning, and developing an academic mindset—a belief in one's ability to grow."[16] Educators readily agree about the importance of the Four Cs or the deeper learning competencies. While many teachers strive to embed some or all of them into their instruction, a focus on standardized assessments, stresses over pacing guides and time available for instruction, and teacher-directed learning can all get in the way of a robust implementation of these skills.

Personalized learning provides many different opportunities to address the Four Cs through a wide range of instructional strategies, and interestingly, incorporating the Four Cs can be an important strategy related to learner agency. Asking students to think critically, to collaborate, to communicate, and to be creative can provide them with ways to drive and have ownership over their work.

Recognize Digital Learning as Integral to Personalized Learning

You can personalize learning for students without digital learning, but realistically, scaling personalized learning for every student in your school without digital learning is not likely. That does not mean, however, that every lesson includes technology. Digital learning can accelerate the shift to personalized learning. Digital learning provides more content options, expands the possibilities for integrating the Four Cs, and can promote learner agency. Digital learning can dramatically expand the resources and tools available for teachers while also providing opportunities for efficiency in their own development and implementation. For example, using tools such as Google Forms, Socrative, or Kahoot as a means of formative assessment can help teachers quickly identify students' needs and misconceptions. While we often use the terms *personalized* and *digital learning* together, they can exist on their own. Some of the less effective examples of digital learning may be found when schools purchase programs in which students engage with content through games of skill and drill but do not employ or promote any of the Four Cs. In our work, digital learning plays a critical role in the move toward personalized learning, and we will continue to share the connections between the two.

CREATE YOUR VISION

Understanding the essential components of personalized learning will help as you guide your stakeholders in developing a vision for teaching and learning. Once you have your vision, you will be able to plan and consider several of the components shared. Developing a formal vision for your school is an essential step toward change, but how you communicate that vision is how you make that vision a reality. Sending the vision home on a piece of paper or posting it on the school's website is rarely enough to make the parents, teachers, students, and community members feel as if they are a part of and own the vision for the school. Strategies for engaging stakeholders demonstrate ways of communication, including showing what engagement looks like, holding focus groups to check for understanding, using language that makes sense, and engaging early and often.

Another tangible step you can take is to create individual elevator pitches. Practice these and help others on your team develop and rehearse theirs. Your elevator speech should be a thirty-second message showcasing the highlights of your vision. Leaders often work arduously through the process of creating the vision, but they may not pause to think about how to communicate their vision in informal settings. Unplanned or quick conversations with parents, business leaders, or community members can represent some of the most uninterrupted and spontaneous opportunities for you to share your vision. Practicing your elevator speech and encouraging your teachers to develop their own can be important in building ownership during planning and implementation. Ensuring that the shared vision is articulated using common language eliminates confusion and instills confidence in a united front presented by the school.

Erin developed her own elevator speech to explain what was important to her and her school:

> Imagine a school where students take ownership of their learning experience and their school environment. A school where students use technology and learn through collaboration with their peers. Where students are not only assessed on their understanding of content, but on their ability to apply their knowledge to solve real-world problems. New Tech West is reimagining education to provide engaging experiences for our students. New Tech West is a small school where students collaborate on projects that require critical thinking, creativity, and communication.

This brief description provides a picture of what learning looks like and what is important to New Tech West. Thinking about this and practicing it ahead of time prepares leaders and teachers for the opportunity to share constructively.

Creating the vision allows you to begin many of the important discussions for implementation. You should not and cannot do this alone, and you will find many strategies to work with others through the stakeholders and leadership chapters.

TRY IT TOMORROW

1. **Provide an opportunity to discuss what teaching and learning should look like.** At a faculty meeting, ask the teachers to develop a visual representation of teaching and learning. Use the prompt "What do you want teaching and learning to look like for our students in two to three years?" and have groups of four teachers create a visual to share their thinking. This might be a picture or a cluster of words. You could also invite a group of students from one or two classes to collaborate in small groups on the same question. Lastly, invite parents to a parent-teacher association or school improvement team meeting, with or without students, to consider the same prompt. This can be a beginning point or a refining point for developing a shared vision.

2. **Practice your elevator speech.** Relaying information about the vision is complicated, and it is essential that the information you put out there makes sense. Principals seem to run into parents, teachers, and community members for short periods of time, and these are perfect opportunities to pitch the speech. Yet principals and teachers rarely set aside the time needed to refine the thirty-second elevator speech. You can practice your own elevator speech and then share it with some of your team. You could also have your staff practice their own at a faculty meeting, something you may want to do with them. One approach could be to let people think about or plan their elevator speech for five minutes. Using a timer, have each person walk around and share it with another person, get feedback, listen to the other person's speech, provide feedback, and then repeat this process with at least two additional people.

2

Engage Stakeholders from the Beginning, but Don't Stop There!

I never refer to anything as "mine" or "my." It's always "our" school when I'm talking to students—or anyone. Sometimes, I call it "your" school. I say it's their school, and I just happen to be the principal. I use those words purposefully. At 7:15 this morning, I was greeting kids, and I do that every day. I go outside and wish them a good day at the end of the day. It's important for your principal to know you and know who you are.

—JOHN BERNIA

An important part of a school leader's work is engaging stakeholders. A good leader creates an environment where teachers, parents, and students feel they are on the same team, working toward the same goals. During the transition toward personalized and digital learning, the need to include stakeholders is stronger than it has ever been before. The reason for this need is two-fold. First, schools are moving in a different direction from the traditional model most of us experienced. Few of us have lived personalized learning in a school setting. Stakeholders, especially parents, community members, and even teachers, may hold onto their own educational experience because "it worked for me." Pulling away from something that worked and moving toward something new can be frightening. Engaging stakeholders in the change process can help overcome some of that fear. Second, many stakeholders are afraid to incorporate digital learning or technology because these things threaten the traditional role of the teacher. Stakeholders who are anxious about such changes need to be reassured that individualized education doesn't mean isolation for their students. Engaging stakeholders in the process of change creates an understanding of how personalization involves learners in the process of designing their own learning path. These misconceptions, anxieties, and fears inhibit the stakeholders' understanding of the need for change. Leaders who are most successful in bringing about change in their school communities understand that they need many strategies and an ongoing plan for involving stakeholders in a meaningful and productive way.

Michael Fullan's recent work related to principals, *The Principal: Three Keys to Maximizing Impact*, emphasizes the importance of the school leader as a change agent, but also points to the role of lead learner to create a collaborative environment for educators and stakeholders and the need to be part of the bigger district system.[1] As lead learners, principals must model that they are always learning and connecting to others who can help them learn in areas that they need or want to grow in as they learn alongside their teachers. Principals are often working to build ownership in a vision that teachers or parents have not seen in action, using technology resources and tools that change quickly. This rapid pace of change requires principals to be more adaptable and more comfortable in modeling their use of technology while also accelerating the school's readiness for change. How do principals engage stakeholders to develop and articulate a shared vision, establish a culture in which taking risks and trying new things is encouraged, model digital learning within their own work, and adapt to the much faster pace of change?

Superintendent Mark Edwards, the 2013 National Superintendent of the Year, led Mooresville Graded School District in North Carolina from 2007 to 2016 with a vision focused on "Every Child, Every Day." He approached his transition to digital learning very differently in Mooresville than he had several years previously in his work with Henrico County Public Schools in Virginia. In Henrico County, he led a one-to-one laptop initiative. The initiative was one of the first and one of the largest laptop deployments of its time. In Henrico County, however, the conversation with stakeholders was much more about laptops than about teaching and learning. In Henrico, back in the early 2000s, school board members, parents, and teachers questioned the "why" of adopting the technology. Shifts in pedagogy and a movement toward student-centered learning were not the primary focus in this laptop initiative. Among stakeholders, the constant focus was on the negatives of using laptops and the problems they caused. The focus was on the technology, not the teaching and learning. Stakeholders got caught up in how laptops were being broken or stolen, or how students might have the ability to access inappropriate content. Part of this negative focus was timing, because this was an early effort for wide-scale technology use, and part of it was a lack of stakeholder buy-in and involvement. This lack of buy-in was likely precipitated by the urgency of getting the effort started and the technology in the hands of teachers and students before laying the groundwork with stakeholders. Stakeholders did not necessarily feel that they were a part of building the effort. This move likely led to those involved feeling as if this effort was done "to them" rather than "with them." Although you can likely relate to the need to move forward quickly while keeping everything else moving, not stopping to work through the process with stakeholders and influencers can come with a significant cost.

Mooresville, North Carolina, is considered a national leader in the work of personalizing learning. Dr. Edwards's approach looked very different here. The results they experienced are very different in terms of culture and stakeholder buy-in. Involving a broad range of stakeholders from the beginning was one of Dr. Edwards's key strategies in Mooresville, and this involvement is consistent with research on organizational change and the examples of effective implementations of personalized and digital learning across the country. In Mooresville, Dr. Edwards engaged an extensive parent committee from the beginning. He ensured, by vote, that 85 percent of his teachers were on board and ready to move toward personalized learning. He worked closely with the school board and led with professional learning. Dr. Edwards and his team put forth the idea of a digital conversion rather than a one-to-one initiative. Their active parent advisory group not only provided critical input to the school and district leaders but also served as the eyes and ears of the schools and district in the community or at the bus stops. Dr. Edwards's chief technology officer and principals were part of the visioning, planning, and implementation. Teachers were expected to grow and be open to changing their own teaching practice, and they were provided with ongoing and job-embedded professional learning, including a Summer Institute, to support them in their learning and application of new ideas. Culture was addressed head-on, and those who did not see themselves as being a part of the conversion did not stay in Mooresville. The focus on teaching and learning and the intense stakeholder involvement from the beginning, which continued throughout the work, led to significant and positive changes. Student outcomes improved dramatically, including a nearly 30 percent increase in the graduation rate after five years of the digital conversion, which began in 2007. The Mooresville district has the second highest test scores in the state, despite a 40 percent free and reduced lunch rate and one of the lowest per pupil expenditure rates.[2]

When we consider the dramatic differences in visioning, planning, and implementation between Henrico County and Mooresville and the many other examples of failed initiatives in many districts, a question arises: How do you ensure that teachers, students, parents, and community members see themselves as part of this transition? Involving stakeholders in the visioning process is important, but their substantive involvement cannot stop with an initial overarching vision. It is important to remember that this change is ongoing. Once you have an overarching vision, stakeholders should continue to be engaged in, be ambassadors for, and contribute to the implementation, reflection, and continuous improvement around the vision.

While parents and teachers are often the focus of attention as being primary and important stakeholders, students are key people to include in the visioning and implementation process. Students play a leadership role in showing what teaching and learning look like in their school. Principals should engage students directly by asking questions, soliciting their input, and valuing their feedback. Community members also often hold important roles in the visioning process. *Community* is a broad, encompassing term that can mean different things for different schools. Local businesses and neighborhoods play an important role in the community, and their support can be invaluable. Invite them into the visioning process using PTA and community meetings. Solicit their thoughts and demonstrate that you're listening and that you appreciate their views.

While the core list of stakeholders is consistent across schools and districts, consider whether you should include particular groups or representatives because of your specific context or community. For example, one principal in

North Carolina learned that a lack of access to the Internet outside of school was a hindrance for students, teachers, and parents. In his community, this lack of access quickly led the principal to ask a preacher in a local church to set up a hotspot, almost like an Internet cafe, for students to use after school and on weekends for homework. That hotspot helped those students and parents feel included and heard. Another principal shared how he knew to tap the skills of a prominent high school coach when trying to show teachers what sort of change was possible. Once this coach shared a lesson that focused on digital learning in a faculty meeting, other faculty members were able to see that they could also make changes. In Mooresville, the school district provided local businesses with stickers to display in their windows to demonstrate that students could access the Internet there. The Mooresville Graded School District leaders also partnered with a local apartment complex to utilize the common area for after-school support and access to the Internet. Each of these stakeholder additions made sense for these specific communities, but different innovations may be critical for you. Who do your students and families interact with on a regular basis? What organizations have a long-standing history and solid reputation in your community? What community leaders or citizens do people look to in times of transition? Who understands and can help you explain why moving to personalized and digital learning will help your community by preparing students for college, career, and citizenship? Finally, consider who the doubters are in your community, who could try to stop your efforts and think of specific ways to reach out to them. It's more challenging to include nonsupporters in the visioning process, but all stakeholders are important in this work.

Engaging the stakeholders does not guarantee support. Teachers, parents, and community members may seem resistant or even nonsupportive when new ideas or approaches to teaching and learning emerge. This resistance is often especially true with personalized and digital learning. This aversion to change typically stems from a history of too many initiatives—all of which seem like fads—or from a fear of something different. People fear change, and this is true for teachers, parents, students, and even the community. The ways principals can alleviate some of these fears, however, are based on being open and inviting. Include parents and community members by asking questions *before* presenting the answer or the solution. Invite stakeholders in to tour model classrooms. Engage stakeholders with frequent check-ins and reflections. Principals can make more progress and expand systemic change when various stakeholders are involved in the process from the beginning.

Principals in this book share many ideas on how to engage stakeholders in ways that contribute and improve the planning and implementation process. Engagement with stakeholders must do the following:

1. Be early and often.
2. Make sense; avoid EduSpeak.
3. Include focus groups.
4. Take a field trip.
5. Address misconceptions and fears.
6. Share the good things that are happening.
7. Communicate and communicate more.

BE EARLY AND OFTEN

Principals need to get out in front and take an early lead in the change process. One of the biggest mistakes leaders make is causing stakeholders to feel as if something is being done *to* them instead of *with* them. Teachers, parents, and community members can lose focus on the big picture if they hear about something being implemented *after* the decision has been made. This type of leadership change for you and your school is likely big, and getting comfortable with it will take time. You will make mistakes engaging people. You will make mistakes communicating with people. This is part of the process, and getting comfortable with missteps is essential. Continue to strive for meaningful exchanges with parents and community members. Ask for their input and listen to it. Consider their input as you develop your plans and strategies. Engaging stakeholders *from the beginning* is crucial to stakeholder buy-in. Dedicating time for stakeholder engagement at the beginning of this transition to personalized and digital learning is critical and will save you time later. Provide a mechanism for ongoing input.

One effective approach to involving people early and getting people excited about possibilities is to stage an event to kick off a new planning or implementation effort or to invite people to your school to tour classrooms. Michael Armstrong, former principal at Bugg Creative Arts Magnet School in Wake County, North Carolina, shares his approach on how he helped get his teachers to rethink their teaching strategies as part of a one-to-one personalized learning initiative he was leading. Michael often scheduled events or showcases where he hosted parents or invited teachers and principals from other schools to come in and visit pilot classrooms to see the learning that was taking place and the approaches that his teachers were using to engage students in their learning. The goal of hosting these events was to recognize the efforts that teachers were making, encouraging them to continue the classroom transformations, and to offer both teachers and students an opportunity to talk about the learning that was taking place in the classrooms. The strategy of using showcases helped him gain momentum for the initiative by energizing his staff and helping the school community come together around a singular focus.

> It was important that I created opportunities for teachers to showcase themselves and their students. Because if teachers can do it for the event, then they can do it every day. There is a balance between these two things. If we have events and we have people coming into our classrooms, teachers will just rise to the occasion and then create ways to keep things up. This is one of the greatest things I learned from Principal Muriel Summers at Combs. She would have this great event and say, "You did this on Thursday, and you can do it every day from now on." Events are a really good time to take risks. Just try something; don't worry about scores, and then the events help us move the mindset. There is security in everyone taking a risk on the same day. If we know Thursday everyone is taking a risk, it's security.

Suzanne Lacey, superintendent of Talladega County Schools in Alabama, describes the importance of engaging in conversations with teachers and administrators early and in honoring teacher's voices:

> In Talladega County, we work well together and generate ideas through formal and informal conversations—mostly informal that eventually become more formal. I have built a solid chain—the brain trust—in our central office. As time goes on, the important people at all stages of the process—teachers and administrators—are included in the conversation. We honor and value the teacher voice because they are the boots on the ground. Teachers have learned to be honest and have become confident in the fact that we will listen.

Involving stakeholders early in the process builds an atmosphere of trust and collaboration. Everyone involved feels respected and feels that ideas are heard. This process builds community and brings people together. Because all the stakeholders involved begin to feel supported, they are more willing to try new things and to keep trying them.

MAKE SENSE; AVOID EDUSPEAK

Educators often use an alphabet soup of acronyms, or EduSpeak. In working with stakeholders, especially those who are not educators, speaking clearly and effectively means using language everyone can understand and relate to comfortably. Ideas and questions should be shared in ways that don't hinder a parent or community member from providing input or asking questions. As you begin to ask questions and involve stakeholders, make sure that they understand and feel comfortable asking for clarification. In Sterling Heights, Michigan, which has experienced a growing population of English language learners, John Bernia, former principal of Carleton Middle School, shares how he used the *Dinner Table Test* to ensure that stakeholders can truly understand and engage in the discussion. "If it makes sense to families who don't work in schools when they sit down for a meal, we've communicated our ideas clearly. 'Making sense' is not necessarily synonymous with 'agreement.' Not every idea we have will meet total support, but the ideas have to make sense."

One way to help your stakeholders make sense of what you're talking about is to show them; don't just tell them. This is an important step in helping stakeholders make sense of where your vision is taking them. We often use videos of examples of school districts, like Mooresville, New Tech West, or Talladega, to allow stakeholders to have a common experience to talk about and to discuss. Sharing more than one example can emphasize that there is not only one right answer to the question of how to implement personalized learning and that we need to find the approach that makes sense for each school. Examples like these are also inspiring for many people because they want to improve education for students but do not feel as though they have the answers as to how. Showing them rather than just talking to them can go a long way. Sharing a video of Talladega, for example, which shares how the district went from a graduation rate of 68 percent to 88 percent (and to 94 percent in 2015), helps them see that the transition to personalized and digital learning takes hard work but is possible. This approach also provides a safe space for discussion and analysis, as leaders, teachers, students, parents, and the community members can talk about another district without criticizing or questioning their own. Taking a group to visit a school where the transition is underway and beginning to lead to positive outcomes provides an authentic experience in which teachers can ask other teachers questions, or a parent could ask other parents how this new technique has worked for their children. Helping stakeholders and influencers see the possibilities, while giving them a common experience to discuss, can allow people to finally see what you mean when you describe personalized learning. This is yet another effort for which the bang for the buck can be huge and well worth the investment of time and resources up front to engage stakeholders.

INCLUDE FOCUS GROUPS

One way to garner feedback or to check for understanding from stakeholders is to conduct focus groups. While focus groups may sound like a research or business approach, they are a useful tool for school leaders. You may already bring together groups of parents through coffees or school improvement team meetings. You can use these gatherings as opportunities to garner more tangible and useful data. Focus groups typically consist of eight to ten individuals charged with addressing specific questions. Allow the conversation in a focus group to flow naturally, without trying to respond to every comment or question. When you're a moderator, your job is to listen and make sure everyone is heard. Focus groups can help clarify an already formulated idea or help develop an idea. Interestingly, focus groups can also be an important step in building ownership of the work itself. People feel as though they have a space to share their voice and contribute to the ideas and the vision.

Summit Public Schools, initially based in California and now expanded to Washington, have utilized focus groups to get frequent and consistent feedback while rolling out their approach to personalized learning. Leaders gathered teachers and/or students on a weekly basis to see how different aspects of the personalized learning approach were working, focusing on content, instructional strategies, or accessibility of data. They asked more general questions about what was working and what could be improved. This method provided a real-time feedback loop with stakeholders directly invested in the process and allowed changes to be made in a timely manner. Teachers and students understood that their input was valued, which also built ownership in the work.[3]

Principals and district leaders can initiate focus groups to learn about perceptions and culture. Culture is the foundation of your school, and understanding the culture is key in bringing about change. Utilizing focus groups from the beginning of the change process can help ascertain helpful information about the culture of the school while also building buy-in and getting important feedback. While you have many conversations each day with teachers and students, asking them to come and share their thoughts on a particular topic can help you see things from a different perspective. We have yet to meet a principal who did not have an "Aha" moment during a focus group with students or teachers. The challenge of not responding, answering questions, or defending choices is always present during a focus group. We often remind leaders in their work with school or district teams or when leading focus groups of Stephen Covey's advice: "Most people do not listen with the intent to understand; they listen with the intent to reply."[4] Focus groups provide a specific space to practice this behavior while also engaging with stakeholders in a meaningful way.

Whether you choose to tap into an existing group or bring together a different group of parents, community members, teachers, or students, you can take several steps to make the focus group more productive:

1. Invite the group for a clearly delineated time period (one hour).
2. Ensure that the group understands the purpose of the focus group and the topic being discussed.
3. Develop a set of clear questions that you would like to ask (five to six are enough for an hour).
4. Record the discussion. Let the people in the room know that the discussion will be recorded but remain confidential.
5. Have the recording transcribed for analysis (or have an avid note-taker with you).
6. Analyze and code the data based on a few designated categories of interest to you.

Analyzing and coding the focus group discussion can be helpful. Choose a few categories, such as challenges and opportunities; culture, pedagogy, and digital resources; or home access, school connectivity, and community supports. Your categories will depend on the focus of the discussion. Once you have established the categories, highlight in different colors and separate your information based on the categories you set up. After you synthesize that information, you have data you can use in your next steps.

Many principals have found that the act of holding a focus group makes parents, teachers, students, and community members realize that you value their input. Being open and listening to understand are important skills to apply here. The Ten Top Tips for Great Focus Groups provide more specific support for conducting focus groups.[5]

TAKE A FIELD TRIP

While principals and teachers can share information about instruction and student work through newsletters or even presentations, having a chance to see teaching and learning in action has great value for stakeholders being asked to create and implement a vision for teaching and learning. After moving to a new school in the Rowan-Salisbury County Schools in North Carolina, principal Derek McCoy recognized that his staff needed support in meeting the new standards and the needs of the students in his school. He also realized that everyone in his school was not necessarily ready or eager to move in this new direction. Rather than try to tell them what they should or could do, he took a team of ten teachers to visit a school in South Carolina that was already making significant gains in student outcomes through experiential learning.

> I took a group of teachers to see a school in South Carolina, and they saw entirely different teaching and learning. The school's leader is the South Carolina Principal of the Year. They do experiential learning, which is totally student-centered. This school was a great place to visit because our teachers could see the power of student-centered learning and true facilitation. After this visit, those ten teachers participated in a fishbowl discussion. That discussion changed the culture of our school. That was one of the most powerful days that I've experienced as an educator. You hear about teachers leading the revolution, but my teachers came back, and they were on fire. Seeing that example helped motivate those teachers. Now, they buy into it. That's what they are going to build.

Derek strategically chose which of his teachers to take with him. He deliberately chose to take not only the most eager teachers and the teachers most ready to change but also some who were more unsure and more nervous about the transition. When all of the teachers experienced what was possible for students, they wanted that experience for their own students. Having teachers see what is possible dramatically accelerated the shift in culture and the transition to personalized learning.

Talladega County Schools, under Suzanne's leadership, has implemented personalized learning across the district, beginning in 2008, and shows what is possible by inviting others into those schools. Their effort began with one high school, Winterboro High School, with a focus on project-based learning supported by technology. The graduation rate for Talladega increased from 62 percent in 2008 to 94 percent in 2015. A significant part of this work is building understanding among teachers and students, as well as the school board and other community members. Talladega County principals invite the community, school board members, and parents into the schools often to see what personalized learning looks like and means for students. Suzanne describes the importance of site visits:

> I think the most significant strategy—still today, over an eight-year jour-ney—is that seeing is believing. We share a lot, but the most convincing thing that we do is have them visit. They need to come and see first-hand what is happening in our schools, and kids need to be leading the charge. That is one of our best marketing tools. In my travels, I see my role as getting stakehold-ers on board. And I can do that, but I tell them they must come for a visit because truly, in a thirty-minute presentation, I cannot give them the truest representation. Most, especially businesses, think school is still the same as it was decades ago. But for them to come and for students to lead and explain their learning is very powerful.

Inviting stakeholders garners support for the continued growth of the effort and also provides specific examples that these stakeholders have seen with their own eyes and can share. The community and school board members become ambassadors for the work within and beyond the district. Similarly, Talladega County visits and learns from other districts across the country. Suzanne makes it a priority to seek out and find opportunities that allow Talladega educators and administrators to be learners in visiting with other districts. Make it a priority for your teachers and stakeholders as well. Schools and other principals will be flattered that you want to visit. Some schools that are asked frequently have set up visiting days. The Charlotte-Mecklenburg School District invites visitors into their Personalized Learning schools, and Mooresville Graded School District leads tours and offers a conference each summer.

ADDRESS MISCONCEPTIONS AND FEARS

Resistance or even apathy from stakeholders is often grounded in miscon-ceptions and fears. Digital learning and technology tend to bring out these fears even more intensely than some other changes to teaching and learning. Teachers may fear that computers will replace them. Headlines like "Technology over Teachers" that emerged in Idaho many years ago when teacher layoffs coincided with a state investment in technology exacerbate that fear. Once teachers see that their role is vitally important in personalized and digital learning, and that they are likely to get to spend more time focused on students and instruction, they can begin to understand that their jobs are not in jeopardy. Teaching may look different because teachers may have opportunities to team teach and significantly change to a more student-centered rather than teacher-directed approach.

Concerns over screen time and child safety often rise to the top, especially if parents, community or board members, or teachers do not have an understanding of what personalized and digital learning can and should be. Parents often fear what students will have access to online and how much time students will be spending online rather than working with a teacher or collaborating with others. Parents are often more afraid of devices replacing teachers than the teachers themselves are. Schools that are moving to personalized learning can help allay these fears by showing parents how each student's experience will actually be more personalized and may include more small group or one-on-one interaction with the teacher. In terms of helping parents see the goals and possibilities of personalized learning, showing and not simply telling can go a long way. Having a group of parents visit a school with other stakeholders, showing videos of exemplars, leading activities to help create the shared vision, and allowing parents to ask questions in a safe setting can address the fears and misconceptions about the importance of the teacher and the concerns about screen time.

Concerns about child safety must be addressed directly with parents, as well as with district and school staff members. Tools and resources to address safety concerns should be available on the school network. Some parents, as well as some school and district leaders and teachers, want to race to filter out a great deal of content and access. However, doing so may not be the most helpful approach for students and their safety. Schools and school devices are not the only places or ways that most students access the Internet and online content. Consequently, we need to discuss and model the idea of digital citizenship. Digital citizenship goes beyond issues of access and helps students understand how to act responsibly online. Students need to learn how to interact and access information online safely, legally, and responsibly at school, where they have heavy filters, as well as in an unfiltered environment elsewhere. Digital citizenship includes what students should do if they encounter a site or individual(s) online with material that is not appropriate or is even dangerous. Common Sense Media is a national leader in supporting schools, districts, and families in teaching and practicing digital citizenship.[6] This organization provides courses and resources for parents, teachers, and students. Many states and even countries have enacted standards for technology, digital learning, and/or digital citizenship. Some are taught in a specific class, whereas others may be addressed through a content area, library media, or guidance. Helping parents to understand what digital citizenship is and how the school and teachers will ensure that students have ongoing and consistent education and reinforcement and application of skills will help alleviate these fears. Parents also appreciate learning how to support digital citizenship and safety at home because many are worried even before the discussion of online access emerges at school.

Inviting people into the school can be one strategy for addressing misconceptions or fears about the use of technology in school. Amy Rickard, principal of Morris Grove Elementary School, invites stakeholders in to see that the use of tools that support personalized and digital learning does not mean students will be on the computer, learning independently, all of the time. Instead of inviting parents to see only students' final products or presentations, Morris Grove Elementary teachers also invite parents to be a part of academic showcases. Parents actively participate in the students' digital learning, participating in activities, games, or other learning experiences that are regularly a part of their students' days. Amy says,

> Helping parents see what their kids are doing and what they are capable of is important. Teachers find ways to showcase what the students are doing. Sometimes, we have to show parents how we use technology because parents are critical to ensuring support for the effort. We have parents who don't want the student to use Google Apps. The school instructional technology facilitator was able to share what Google Apps was like for kids and how it allows kids to collaborate with teachers. It's helping parents who are not aware to understand that when we roll out Google Apps, the kids are still in

a bubble and we have protocols. You have to answer individual parents and help to educate.

Taking time early in the process to answer questions and acknowledging concerns can help build trust with stakeholders and often avoid hurdles later in the implementation. Being explicit and making sure that parents understand how and why certain things are happening work hand-in-hand with ongoing stakeholder engagement.

SHARE THE GOOD THINGS THAT ARE HAPPENING

Education news stories often point out negative happenings at a school or focus on grades or test scores. School leaders have an opportunity to share the good things that are happening on a regular basis. This kind of sharing drives the story of the change to personalized learning and provides more examples of what is possible for students. This approach brings positive press to the school, puts out accurate information, and boosts morale for teachers and students because they see their work recognized and appreciated. Take time to highlight the amazing things your teachers and students are doing. By pointing out the commitment of the school and teachers to helping students reach their potential, you help engage stakeholders and create some of your biggest supporters.

Tim Lauer utilized social media to share the teaching and learning happening while he was principal at Meriwether Lewis Elementary School. Although some of the things he highlighted were special or eventful, most were everyday snapshots of teaching and learning. Tim communicated through a multitude of different media, ensuring a consistent online presence:

> It's really important to highlight the good work taking place. Around the country, a lot of local media approach schools and education as adversarial. They do like the occasional ribbon cutting and smiling, but [they] know what gets page views and comments is associated with finance. If we leave it up to local media, they will skew the picture a little bit; but we need to tell our story, too. Tell it authentically. Highlight the commitment of the students and teachers.
>
> It is interesting to look at the parent community and how they engage in social media. Facebook, for most families, is where we get most engagement. There are different audiences for different platforms. People who follow on

Twitter, in terms of school community, are more technical folks. Facebook is more "mom and pop"—where moms and dads go to share family information, and they like to engage with school in that way. You have different audiences in mind with how people like to get to their media. You have to be aware of that and not think that only one channel is going to get you access to all the families.

Tim's use of social media garnered support from his district by getting the word out to community members, board members, and parents. He led by example, but then also made it easy for them to reshare what he was posting. This method helped his school, as well as the other schools in the district. According to Tim,

The school district has really stepped up to share good news around the district. They've been really good about engaging administration and teachers already active in these spaces. There has been a change in thinking. It used to be more central control with one message, but we realized that social media breaks that down. Rather than fight it, they've embraced it, so they retweet and share. They home-grow some content, but also share other content from schools, principals, and teachers. This isn't a PR spin. This is Ms. Smith who posted this cool picture about the art project. School board members are active on Facebook and part of that is because of politics, but they do use it as a way to engage community that they wouldn't have five years ago.

While engaging stakeholders can involve many different facets and can take time and energy, it leads to more efficient and effective implementation of new ideas. This type of sharing also addresses some of the challenges discussed in this chapter. When parents see examples of students collaborating, with or without technology, they are more comfortable with the transition to personalized and digital learning. When they are able to see what learning can be for their children, they realize that personalized learning does not simply mean being in front of a computer. When students explain what being a digital citizen means, they teach parents and also make parents more confident in their child's ability to navigate being online. Parents and community members want to believe in their schools, so they can become your biggest advocates by sharing the positive news and examples. Identifying the key stakeholders in your community and choosing ways to engage them early and often can make a big difference in garnering support, developing understanding, and ensuring sustainability.

COMMUNICATE AND COMMUNICATE MORE

Communication is essential in each aspect of the engagement process. While you have a school to lead and run, you can help all aspects of what you do by communicating often and in different ways to reach your many stakeholders. Clearly, this cannot be the only thing you do, but if you develop clear structures and other ongoing ways to share, you can build this activity into your daily work. Tim posted pictures or short video clips as he walked through classrooms on a regular day. He did not wait for the culminating project or the end of the quarter. He shared what teaching and learning looked like every day at Meriwether Lewis Elementary. Michael included video clips as part of his newsletter to parents. While many of you have your own newsletters, and may even have an additional PTA newsletter, think about ways to make it more interactive. Pictures are certainly a start, but can you include student voices, through writing or video, and show what happens every day in your school? That is what your vision and education are about—the *in-the-moment* exchange of ideas and creation of new products.

You may want to mix it up. Some districts have an every-Sunday call that leads and ends with the same message each week. While consistency is good, it also creates a numbness to the message. If you highlight different students, teachers, or classes or ask questions for feedback, you may get more attention than always ending with a repeat of the dress code. Parents and students want to hear what is happening uniquely in their school, how the vision that they (ideally) played a role in developing is being implemented, and how they can engage with their students at home or school in a more meaningful way. You may also need to go beyond e-mails or phone calls and be present where your community lives. Attend festivals or other events and let people know through conversation what is happening. You can't do this every week, but making an effort once a quarter or semester can go a long way. Hold parent meetings at a pizza place or in an apartment complex's common space. Offer to share or attend Kiwanis Club or Chamber of Commerce meetings. Once community members or parents who are active in the community hear where you are going, they will want to support you, especially if you are sharing why learning matters and what this work means for kids. Meet parents and community members where they are—for discussion, for creating a shared vision, and for continuous improvement.

TRY IT TOMORROW

1. **Conduct a focus group with teachers, parents, students, or community members.** Pose a new question you've been thinking about, or task them with developing an idea that's already in place. You could conduct sessions with all these stakeholders, but simply starting with one group is a great first step.

2. **Invite stakeholders into the school to see personalized learning in action.** Keep it simple. Work with one or two teachers to invite parents or community members into the classroom to see a specific process in action. After a visit to the classroom, debrief with the stakeholders, pointing out how the learning they saw in action connects to the school's vision, as well as the benefit of the instruction for the students.

3. **Plan a site visit to a school in your district, region, or state that is implementing personalized and digital learning.** Start close to home and with a small group of teachers. Reach out to a school that is doing something you admire and would like to investigate further.

4. **Identify two ways to highlight positive things happening in your school this week.** Determine a couple of ways to show something good happening with teaching and learning in your school this week. Like Tim Lauer, you could post a picture or short video clip of teaching and learning happening. You can do this immediately. You can also include a video clip highlight of the week in your Friday note. Use a tool like Adobe Voice, Adobe Spark, Tackk, or Pic Collage to create something that looks professional without performing a lot of complicated steps.

3

Employ Change Management and Distributed Leadership

As a leader, my role isn't to be the one with all the answers. My call is to create the space and time for our staff to learn, to connect people with colleagues who can help them, to ask quality questions, and to ensure our teachers have what they need to incorporate instructional technology into their practice. Classroom teachers who are "doing the work" in their classrooms have a far better command of what works and what doesn't in classrooms. I have to listen, encourage, observe, ask, and support.

—JOHN BERNIA

EMPLOY CHANGE MANAGEMENT

As you are acutely aware, principals are the only ones in their buildings with their job. Sometimes this fact leads principals to think that they need to handle a great deal on their own because no one else understands or no one else has the skill set or responsibility. However, you cannot bring about change on your own. If you work in a vacuum, the transition and progress you make will end after you leave the building, if it ever gets off the ground at all. Making the transition to personalized and digital learning requires fundamental—not incremental—change. This work is about helping the many stakeholders involved see new possibilities that require them to leave their comfort zone to be effective. Leadership must be purposeful. When you talk with people who think that things just happen or people will simply follow, you will rarely find someone who has buy-in, ownership, and a shared vision among the teachers, parents, students, and community members.

The collaborative nature of your role as a leader makes understanding leadership and change management incredibly important. Once you see your role in the transition as leading a change *process*, you will be able to pinpoint the many steps to take in doing this work. Engaging stakeholders in creating a vision and keeping them engaged throughout the entire planning and implementation process are critical steps in change management. But the work does not stop there. You will use change management and distributed leadership as tools and guides throughout your work.

DISTINGUISH CONSENSUS VERSUS MOMENTUM

One distinction that is interesting to consider—and it takes guts to really grapple with this concept—is the difference between consensus and momentum. Consensus is the agreement and unity that exist around an idea. Momentum is the strength or force that something has when it's moving. Principals often work with hundreds or even thousands of stakeholders. Ensuring that everyone has a shared vision and shared involvement in planning and implementation is important, but you must understand that not every person has to be in complete agreement. Achieving a full consensus on every issue with all stakeholders involved will be impossible. It is often more important to achieve a consensus *of sorts* and to keep moving forward to develop momentum for the changes you are looking to implement.

At Bugg Creative Arts Magnet School, former principal Michael Armstrong utilized management expert W. Edwards Deming's research in his own thinking as a reminder to *strive for momentum*:[1]

> What anchors me is Edwards Deming. So many problems we focus on in schools cannot be solved through consensus. Real change comes from momentum. Momentum is the spirit of the group. If you have one hundred teachers and you are trying to start a new program, instead of trying to get all one hundred on board, try to find ten that are excited about the program. Work with those ten and get started with the program. You will then have ten contagious people, championing the new program and that energy will spread. Principals try to make it even, but sometimes those you empower can empower others.

Deming's research helps make building momentum and working toward a shared vision for personalized and digital learning seem more feasible. You have involved the critical stakeholders in the visioning process. The next step is to make this vision a reality. Deming advised managers to focus on the square root of the size of a team or staff rather than on building consensus with the entire staff. You could think of parents, students, or community members in a similar way. For example, if you have a staff of thirty-six people, you need only the square root of thirty-six—six individuals—to build momentum. Those six stakeholders will go out and work to increase the base. For high schools, you may have closer to one hundred staff members, so you need ten for momentum. It is worthwhile to consider who those six or ten people are (or whatever number corresponds with your school). These individuals may be in different roles. They may include a library media specialist, a social studies teacher who is also a coach, a literacy specialist, and a fourth-grade teacher.

Similarly, you also should consider the *momentum builders* among your parents, students, and community members. Identifying and focusing on this momentum-building group will allow you to move forward with the vision in a more effective way as you are distributing leadership—building and empowering leaders—in your school. These people will model for and communicate with other teachers, students, parents, and community members. In planning and identifying your potential leaders, you should not simply assume that those with a love for digital learning will be the best momentum builders. Don't assume that those who are always the first to volunteer will be the best ambassadors for this sort of change. Sometimes, a leader is an individual who has a need or connection to why personalized and digital learning will help a child. Sometimes it is someone who is ready to take on a new leadership role in the school. Be creative in identifying these momentum builders because they are such an important factor in bringing about real change.

Principal Troy Moore explains how he approached his role in creating change and also how he supported leadership among his team in building personalized learning at his previous school in Charlotte–Mecklenburg:

> I approach my role as the torchbearer. I try to run ahead and lead on research and vision, to shed light on the possibilities for our students and staff. Some people call this the lead learner, but I like the concept of equity among colleagues. I see my staff as colleagues. We are all in the trenches together. I

see the torchbearer not as quietly creeping through a dark cave but inspiring others to prepare to strategically storm the hill and make a difficult climb full of adversity.

Personally, I thrive on colleagues that I call early adopters. These teachers are impassioned about doing all they can to promote student success and are waiting to try out the next best instructional strategy to try in their classroom. Inspiring early adopters is incredibly rewarding work for a school leader. The school leader can visualize what innovative instruction should look like, provide the PD [professional development], provide the resources/time to develop, and even get in the classroom to model it; but ultimately it is the early adopter colleagues who make it happen. Once inspired, they implement, refine, and spread the good word about the strides they are making for students in their learning environment.

During my tenure as principal of Hawk Ridge Elementary in Charlotte, North Carolina, I had a dynamic group of colleagues who moved mountains in the classroom. What we accomplished together in two years within the personalization of learning for our students was amazing. The most rewarding comments I have ever heard in my entire educational leadership career were when some of my teachers said to me, "Troy, I could never teach in a school that does not seek to personalize the learning for their students after what I have now been a part of." In a nutshell, my role in the transition to personalization is to be a lead researcher, an inspirer of early adopters, a developer of a safe environment for risk taking, and an intentional listener for roadblocks that need to be cleared.

PRACTICE DISTRIBUTED LEADERSHIP

Transitioning to personalized and digital learning ultimately involves organizational change and an understanding of the essential components, pitfalls, and strategies to manage and lead the change successfully. Principals must be able to adapt to a much more expedient pace of change with digital content, data and assessment systems, and technology tools and resources available to support teaching and learning. Principals cannot lead a school, and more specifically cannot lead a transition to personalized and digital learning, by themselves. This realization goes beyond the simple reality of the workload. The importance of distributed leadership builds on the need for ownership in the school, building on strengths and offering opportunities to teachers and other staff members who are seeking additional roles. Principals who lead adaptable and sustainable transitions to digital learning do the following:

- build leaders to ensure distributed leadership
- develop hybrid roles for teachers
- hire thoughtfully
- model personalized and digital learning

Build Leaders to Ensure Distributed Leadership

Do you have a teacher, an instructional coach, or a media coordinator that you see as part of your leadership team not just in name, but truly in leading the school? Nearly every principal we asked about leading an effective transition to personalized and digital learning quickly pointed to, without being prompted, several other leaders in the school who were integral to the success of the transition. Along with engaging stakeholders, identifying and building leaders within your own school are essential aspects of leading a transition to personalized and digital learning. You cannot be everything to everyone, and you certainly cannot be everywhere you likely will need to be at the same time. This distributed leadership approach is consistent with the approaches of the principals highlighted in this book. These principals all begin with a belief that they cannot bring about change single-handedly. They all are savvy enough to recognize the strengths in other stakeholders and confident enough to empower those stakeholders as leaders.

A key piece of distributed leadership is a willingness to look beyond the traditional administrative or leadership titles. Strong and effective leaders are not always the people who hold official titles in a school or a community. As we look at schools across the country that have been successful in their transition to personalized and digital learning, we see schools with leadership teams that include coaches, media coordinators, and instructional technology facilitators who are empowered to bring forward new ideas to reach the school's vision. In some cases, even with the human resource challenges often found in public school systems, new roles are created with titles that signal a shift in the focus and vision of the particular school.

Michael approached his leadership team with an openness to their interests and strengths:

> You have to know your people. That sounds so cliché, but really know what makes them excited and what makes them spark. [One teacher] loved working with adults, so when she got to do that, it was magical. A teacher of gifted and

special education loved both, so we created a job where she could do both. At the end of each year, I ask people what their dream job would be and then try to create dream positions. If people are doing what they are excited about, it will work!

In his public high-need elementary school, Michael created a dean of academics and a dean of professional development. These positions helped show the importance of curriculum and instruction and also helped ensure professional development was part of every day. Creating these positions helped Michael have other leaders who felt responsible for the vision of the school and its implementation. When we visited his school, it was quickly apparent that Michael was not the only one who could speak to and lead discussions about where the school was and where it was going. The teachers now had other leaders with whom they could share ideas and seek out support when they needed help.

Setting up this support structure is particularly helpful with the implementation of personalized and digital learning because teachers need significant support to understand what this new culture could look like and how and where they might begin. The dean of professional development, for example, not only coached teachers throughout the week but also held targeted professional development sessions every Monday so that teachers could participate during their planning times. During the professional development, teachers had the chance to be immersed in personalized and digital learning that was then followed up by collaborative coaching sessions. Classroom observations, teacher needs assessments, and other data were used to determine the focus of the Monday sessions. This position provided a clear leader in the school who focused on professional learning and used data and follow-up to determine the most critical needs of the staff. While these are not typical roles, they met the needs of this school to move toward its vision for teaching and learning and capitalized on the strengths of its team.

Principal Amy Rickard of Morris Grove Elementary School knows that simply identifying teachers or other people in the building as leaders is not always enough to help them see themselves as leaders. She strives to empower teachers, while making a very conscious choice to engage many of them over time rather than always relying on the few others who naturally volunteer and are comfortable with the role:

> You have to know your teachers and use every opportunity to get to know your teachers and their strengths, needs, and interests. You are that conduit to moving teachers into leadership roles. You help to create that agency. Some teachers think they are not ready, but it's helping them to see it and take those leadership roles. I had a mentor who had a rule that you could not hold a leadership role for more than two years. That was especially true in high school. So, I thought I would do that here. The leadership team, SIT members, and others rotate, creating a culture where not one person is the expert on a certain team.

Your staff can become complacent or feel stifled if the same people are continuously tapped for leadership roles. Thinking about how to continually help people grow, while also offering opportunities to a broad range of staff members and teachers, is important to building truly distributed leadership.

Principal Erin Frew, formerly of New Tech West High School, specifically sought out those who could complement her strengths and weaknesses and also push her thinking. Her view of distributed leadership represents the importance of thought partners in this work:

> I try to be as distributed and collaborative as possible. I'm very thoughtful about how people are used, capitalizing on their strengths and acknowledging where I am not as strong. I have found this builds capacity throughout. For example, I have one staff member whom I trust and respect a great deal. I can count on him to always be the devil's advocate to make sure I am always thinking about the problems. I have another who focuses me on the positive. When I get mired in the minutia, he's good at pointing out where we've been successful. He is helpful with the culture part. He reminds me that we have to have celebrations and think about culture. As a Type A, like most principals, it's something I have really worked on. You can't do it by yourself. There's no way.

Develop Hybrid Roles for Teachers

While developing hybrid roles for teachers is related to understanding and implementing distributed leadership, it is important to specifically consider how developing other options can support retention in a school and also build on the strengths of those already on the team. In a traditional school setting, teachers have jobs that are nearly the same on the first day of their career to the last, and the only way they can take on a new role or new challenge is to move into administration. Many teachers seek out administrator roles, like becoming a principal, simply because other options do not necessarily exist. Others who seek leadership roles while still teaching simply add duties to their already-too-busy schedule. You probably have teachers like this in your building.

Moving to personalized and digital learning leads to significant changes in teaching and learning, which dramatically shifts the teaching role. This move also provides opportunities to keep excellent teachers working directly with students by exploring the possibilities of hybrid roles. MetLife conducted an annual Survey of the American Teacher from 1984 to 2012 and asked questions about leadership roles in the 2012 administration of the survey. Fifty-one percent of teachers shared that they would be interested in hybrid roles in which they could continue to teach at least part time in the classroom while also taking on leadership roles.[2] Currently, teachers who take on extra duties or roles are rarely compensated adequately, and these efforts can contribute to burnout based on workload. With the role of the teacher expanding, your challenge is to create hybrid roles that encourage teachers to expand their leadership and take on new challenges that build on their instructional expertise while also helping them maintain reasonable workloads.

Former principal Tim Lauer discusses how he hired a teacher with a strength in writing and literacy at Meriwether Lewis Elementary School, and he was able to almost immediately provide that teacher with a hybrid role that also met the needs of other teachers in the school:

> One of the teachers I hired is co-director of the Oregon Writing Project. He's been in that role of leadership and leading PD. He brings a lot to the school in that capacity. There's a level of authenticity in what he's saying. He's worked with teachers, and he's really good at being transparent in his practice and showing when things work and don't work. I'm trying to get to that level with my staff. Hire good people and get them resources they need—and get out of the way. You have to have an idea on where you want to go, but know that the road you take will not be set and will change. It's a journey. That's the exciting part, too. You don't know how it's going to end—*and it's not going to end.*

Superintendent Suzanne Lacey involves Talladega County school leaders and teachers in a district-level leadership team to help build the pipeline of leaders and build confidence in teachers in their own leadership capacity:

In Talladega, we have an ongoing professional development commitment which starts with our administrators. At each meeting, they bring a lead teacher. That has been a critical component to developing leaders. Meetings are in a school each time, so part of the process is to visit classrooms and observe through instructional rounds and then reflect and provide feedback to administrators. That has been huge to grow leaders through teachers, but also through administrators.

When you become an administrator, you don't know everything about instruction, so administrators can work with lead teachers in their schools. I often say that teachers just need a stage to perform, and you have to give them that stage and build confidence and trust them in leadership. Through this process, I've seen this happen. When teachers understand the expectations and they learn and share back, they stand a little straighter, feel taller. We have identified so many leaders who didn't know they were leaders. They were good teachers but now see themselves differently.

Talladega's example reminds leaders to include teachers in leadership discussions and bring them along to experience what you do in your role while also sincerely asking for their input. How can you observe more and provide opportunities like this to grow leaders in your school?

Amy mentions that it is easy to rely more heavily on coaches and specialists, but it is important to also allow teachers to have these leadership roles with the coaches or specialists supporting them:

This year, I really tried to shift to using learning-focused lesson planning. Sometimes there is an overreliance with our specialists/coaches, but this year, with the Learning-Focused Lessons, we've sent classroom teachers to be coaches/teacher leaders so they trained the other teachers. It made it feel more doable. We trained people on two teams, instead of everyone. These two PLC [professional learning community] teams have been the leads. This feels less top down. We've had teachers stand up and say this has helped. This made me realize that I need to figure out how to do more of this and build even more formal structures of teacher leadership.

Troy found that growing leaders must be intentional:

Growing leaders demands time. As a leader, if you give them your time, they will see you as a colleague and be more interested in developing visionary implementations. This time comes in the form of after-school discussions, travel to see other schools showing success on the same implementations, targeted staff development planned by the leader, and in class coteaching with the administrator. When we were in development of how to balance teacher direct instruction to the individual within a Personalized Pathway for each student, getting in there and trying it for myself with the teacher was formative in the decision making going forward. I also think ensuring a safe environment for risk taking grows leaders. When teachers are valued for their expertise and trusted, they are inspired to think outside the box and get others on board as well.

Hybrid roles for teachers, especially those with leadership responsibilities, will look different in each school, and it will take purposeful action to create those positions and help teachers see the value you see in them. The transition to personalized and digital learning, however, provides many avenues for new roles. It may allow you to call out the need for additional professional learning or peer mentoring because of the newness of the work. Likewise, you might need to encourage some teachers to be more involved in curriculum development or even policy setting around home access or the use of devices. As you uncover gaps in your own skills or those on your staff and places where you need support and leadership, you can use this development of hybrid roles to help retain teachers, provide avenues for growth, and also be integral to the distributed leadership model.

Hire Thoughtfully

Principals typically inherit a staff when they assume leadership of a school. Whether the principal moves to the role internally or from another school or district, the staff has its strengths and weaknesses, and the school has a culture engendered by the previous leader. Aside from building an effective culture for your transition to personalized and digital learning, you will also likely have the opportunity to slowly (or in some cases more quickly) hire teachers as educators move to a new school, retire, or leave the profession. As you have the opportunity to hire teachers, develop interview questions and even protocols that help you support your school's vision and also complement the faculty and staff currently at the school.

Amy had the opportunity to build her own staff when she opened Morris Grove Elementary in 2007. "When I opened Morris Grove, it was really important to me to not establish a culture of individual 'superstars.' I had previously worked in a school where teachers were really competitive with one another; they would not share resources, were overly concerned about their individual student data, etc." Her initial informal motto was "Leave your ego at the door," because she strongly believed in professional learning communities and teamwork as core to building the culture of the school. She involved her staff in her approach to hiring. "It's important to select staff to dig into that for your interview process, making sure they are a match for you and you are a match for them." Amy uses questions like the following—for teachers, specialists, other instructional support staff, and teacher assistants as noted—to help tease out how candidates approach teamwork and collaboration:

- We have a strong foundation in professional learning communities (PLC) and teachers work tightly within PLC teams to plan for instruction and support student learning. Effective teacher collaboration goes beyond friendly cooperation and the informal exchange of ideas and information. What must effective teacher collaboration include?
- With what kind of teachers do you do your best work? What kind of teacher would be challenging for you in this environment?
- How do you use assessment data to plan for instruction? How have you used data within a PLC team?
- Our schools are based on the professional learning communities framework. Collaboration with other teachers is a major component of this model. Describe the type of working relationships you prefer with a regular education teacher. *(Used for resource [EC, ESOL, Gifted] teachers)*
- One of our philosophies at Morris Grove is that all adults share ownership for all students. Although you will be assigned primarily to one classroom, there are times [when] you may be asked to work with other students or classes. Talk to us about your experiences in working as part of a team. *(Used for teacher assistants)*

Having the team that a candidate will join be a part of the interview process can help garner buy-in and support once a teacher is hired and can expedite the transition to the PLC or team. This is also an opportunity to help your team learn and improve by reflecting on their culture and the type of person they need to complement their strengths and weaknesses and their approach to working together for students. Amy says, "I have also made a couple of hiring decisions where a candidate professed to be collaborative—and it seemed from reference checks that he/she was—only to find out that was not the case. However, they have since moved on, as I think they realized that they could not shift the culture of collaboration that was established. They really wanted to work in isolation, and it became too difficult for them to work in the PLC environment."

Erin asked teaching candidates how they use technology in their personal lives. While recognizing that personal use does not ensure translation into using technology in pedagogy, she found that how candidates approach technology use in terms of creativity and the comfort level with which they describe their day-to-day use are very telling for readiness and openness to using digital learning for project-based and personalized learning. You can also look for references to personalized and digital learning—and alignment to your school's vision—in candidates' responses to more traditional interview questions. Other questions or prompts to consider include the following:

- How do you describe yourself as a learner?
- What role do you typically play on a team or PLC?
- Describe a lesson that you think engaged your students.
- Describe a lesson in which you utilized digital learning.
- How do you meet the needs for students with a wide range of strengths, learning differences, and challenges?
- When you review our vision, what makes you the most excited? What makes you the most nervous?
- What would you like to learn more about in regard to personalized and digital learning?

Other principals ask candidates to prepare and lead a lesson for the grade level of the position for which they are being interviewed. It can be a bit complicated to schedule this lesson or identify the standard or topic that will likely coincide with the class period they will teach. However, you can learn a great deal by observing the lesson, including how the candidates approach personalized and digital learning. Does the use of digital learning change the lesson or simply replace something that could be done on a chalkboard? Is the lesson student-centered? Does the teacher allow for student voice? Does the lesson address the Four Cs? Having one or two others join in the observation could be a learning experience for existing staff members. Of course, these teacher candidates will likely put a great deal into planning the lesson and will also be more nervous than on a typical day of teaching, but you could learn a lot about them by reflecting on the lesson with them to understand the thinking behind certain choices or approaches.

Michael asked potential candidates to prepare a lesson for the grade level they were interviewing for from a list of topics that students had already covered. The lesson was intended to be a review and allowed him and others on the leadership team to get a sense of the potential employees' teaching style and to see how they interacted with students.

Amy involves her current team in the hiring process and also seeks out individuals who will directly support the culture and vision. When you have the opportunity to hire a new teacher, try to ensure that the teacher will enhance the culture of the school and that the strengths and weaknesses will complement the current team or staff and that the school also will help the candidate grow. Investing time in the hiring process provides hybrid opportunities for current team members while ideally helping the school realize its vision for teaching and learning.

Model Personalized and Digital Learning

The importance of modeling is exponentially pronounced when transitioning to personalized and digital learning. This effort includes modeling risk taking and sometimes failing, as well as utilizing digital tools and resources and implementing personalized learning for all learners, both adults and students. Modeling may push you and other leaders out of their comfort zone, but this task can be embedded in daily work, processes, structures, and outreach. You may or may not use a plethora of digital tools or resources in your daily work, but it is likely that you use some on which you can build. If you use Google documents, think about how can you model using this tool to collaborate with educators. Use faculty meetings or other standing meetings as opportunities to practice personalized and digital learning. This way, teachers, parents, and students can see what this means. A simple example is flipping a faculty meeting by having teachers watch a short, thought-provoking video or read a short article before the meeting and then utilizing the faculty meeting time for interactive discussions. The discussions or interactive parts could even use rotational models if you are trying to guide teachers toward more blended approaches. You could use walk-throughs as a means of staying focused and emphasizing the school's vision for teaching and learning. Using digital learning as a way to communicate immediately with teachers during walk-throughs helps build an open, nonthreatening approach to improving teaching and learning while modeling effective uses of technology to personalize the interaction with each teacher.

School leaders can also model important practices in daily interactions. John Bernia, former principal of Carleton Middle School, reminds us to listen:

> The other great lesson that I learned is that I really have to listen to people. If you listen, you will get them there. I think that's where teaching is headed. Teachers are going to have to be really good listeners. When you listen and ask a good question as follow-up, that will generate more discussion. Yes, the Internet will change the game, but it's also going to make teachers more important. The human interaction is key. The teachers that are the best listeners and harness the Internet, digital learning, and technology for the purpose of learning—not teaching—will be the most successful.

Amy models by coaching her lead teachers. She has conversations with them that guide them through a problem-solving approach with their challenges with their team:

> We need to understand and talk about goals for the team and how we grow ourselves as a PLCs. I ask the lead teachers, "What do you need to work on?" I had one team that was really struggling with sharing students and that resisted implementing of CLIMB time, a differentiated, cross-classroom opportunity to focus on specific standards. I took mCLASS data and showed growth of the grade levels below and above, and showed them what was happening with the instructional touches and growth. Encouraging them to look at data and what is working can help make your point. Model the use of data.

Amy uses this approach to model and empower her teacher leaders. She models using data and applying it to personalizing learning while also helping grow coaching and leadership skills.

The bottom line is that you cannot do this work alone. Keep in mind this African proverb: "If you want to go fast, go alone. If you want to go far, go together." Utilizing distributed leadership and hybrid roles and also hiring carefully are critical to making progress in this transition to personalized and digital learning. At the same time, you are more likely to retain effective teachers and other administrators because they see themselves as having true ownership in the vision and implementation of personalized and digital learning. Consequently, you also can create many of the fundamental components necessary for long-term sustainability and adaptability. This task may not be easy in the beginning or may take time to understand who should take on what role, but this will make the work more effective—and almost always, more enjoyable and fulfilling.

TRY IT TOMORROW

1. **Do the square root activity (Deming).** Consider your staff size and compute the approximate square root. Who are your "square root" people? Reflect on how you currently use those momentum builders and whether you have enough or need to identify more. Do you have too many to truly focus your efforts? How might you bring these people together to help build momentum around your shared vision?

2. **Conduct a focus group with teachers about hybrid roles.** Gather a cross-section of teachers in your building, including those who have and those who have not had hybrid roles. Ask questions related to the following:
   a. How do you feel about the opportunities for your own professional growth and roles available in our school?
   b. How do you see your ability to shape your role or career in our school?
   c. What types of opportunities would you like for hybrid roles?
   d. How could hybrid roles be of interest to you, and what types of structures or supports would have to be in place?
   e. How else would you like to see your role evolve?

3. **Review and potentially develop new interview questions and protocols.** If you will be hiring in the near future, consider and review your protocols, interview questions, and even job announcement for how they embody your school's vision for teaching and learning and culture. With a group of teachers and/or staff members, develop questions and protocols that will help support your vision and culture. Here are a few of our favorite interview questions:

- If I were to ask your students, "What is your teacher's biggest weakness," how would they answer?
- Describe a lesson that you recently taught that you think went particularly well.
- How do you use technology to personalize instruction for students during lessons or in projects?
- Describe what a day in your classroom would look like.
- What does a classroom that promotes creativity and learner agency look like? How would you describe the space?

4

Build a Culture of Trust in Which It Is Acceptable to Fail

*Teachers are our most precious resources.
As leaders, we have to do all we can to protect
them, provided they have a growth mindset
and are willing to try new things.*

—TROY MOORE

We've all had the experience of walking into an unfamiliar school, questioning a particular policy or routine, and getting the answer, "That's just the way we do things around here." The way things get done in a school is part of a school's culture. Richard DuFour, Rebecca DuFour, and Robert Eaker further define culture as "the assumptions, beliefs, expectations and habits that constitute the norms for a school."[1] Terrence Deal and Kent Peterson consider culture the "inner reality" of a school.[2] Many educators say you can feel a school's culture as soon as you walk through the front doors, whereas others believe that you need to talk to the teachers, students, and parents before you can really get a sense of it. School culture involves the administrators, teachers, staff, and students, but it also includes parents and the community. All stakeholders are continually involved, consciously or unconsciously, in defining and setting school culture. In our opinion, based on our experience with hundreds of schools, the culture of a school will make or break the success of a transition to personalized and digital learning.

Michael Armstrong, former principal of Bugg Creative Arts Magnet School, makes a point of talking about the difference between culture and climate to ensure that we do not gloss over the deep-seated nature of culture. Climate can be described as the daily mood of the school. Climate can swing up and down, depending on certain variables. The Monday morning after the team's big win may have people feeling happy and celebratory. During a weeklong testing period, the climate may be grumpy or frustrated. While climate can fluctuate daily, the culture of a school remains constant. Culture is sustainable, grounded in the roots of a school and how the school works and functions. An effective culture is what sustains a school when things do not go as planned or people are having a rough day—during climate changes. A strong school culture can dramatically help a school principal who is looking to make some changes.

Examining your school culture to identify its components is necessary before beginning the work of bringing around changes. If the culture is secure, and one in which stakeholders trust you as a leader, teachers, students, and parents will be more willing to follow your suggestions—and more forgiving if some of your ideas don't work. If the culture is toxic, you may have good ideas that many are excited about, but a few negative and questioning voices (often the same ones again and again) will be able to invoke doubt and make others hesitant to jump in and try something. If the culture tends to be rigid and top-down, people may not be comfortable expressing an opinion and will truly fear taking a risk. Many of these scenarios can make the shift toward personalized and digital learning nearly impossible or very impersonalized. Focusing on establishing or affirming an effective culture provides the backbone necessary so that shifts in climate are possible and do not have negative lasting impacts.

Whatever the culture of your school is, it's important to understand that you can't bring about change in an atmosphere of fear. School leaders who are leading transition efforts often discover that teachers and other key stakeholders are afraid to make a mistake, afraid to try new things. Sometimes this fear is the result of not letting certain things go or failing to stop certain practices or areas of focus. For example, if you are asking teachers to embrace project- or problem-based learning (PBL), but you do not free them from district-provided, sometimes rigid pacing guides, the teachers may feel confused and stuck. It is challenging for teachers to take a leap and try something as complex and time consuming as a genuine PBL approach if they are still expected to work in a more linear framework. Fear can also result from a "Gotcha!" attitude in the school. The way that you and the other leaders in the school or district approach walk-throughs and more formal evaluations makes a significant difference in your school's culture. Teachers should see you as someone who wants to help them improve their instruction. They should believe you are all on the same team. If teachers are more worried about your seeing them make a mistake than they are about receiving constructive feedback, the culture in your school is probably not conducive to a transition to personalized and digital learning. You and your teachers need to trust each other through the mistakes; you will all have to take risks together. All stakeholders need to see the transition to personalized learning as a learning process.

Principal Troy Moore, formerly of Hawk Ridge Elementary School, sums it up this way:

> I strive for my teachers to see me as a colleague. I am always seeking transparent conversations where we talk freely about obstacles. It takes time for teachers to believe that an administrator is not going to use something that was said against them.
>
> Teachers have to be trusted until proven otherwise. I love ensuring a safe environment where teachers can be risk takers with something new they saw on Twitter or Pinterest that they think will benefit their students. I love giving teachers the opportunity to own their instructional minutes and have the flexibility to adjust core content blocks daily given what they are teaching. I always say, "There is nothing more powerful than an impassioned teacher! That teacher is going to make it happen for kids!"

Teachers and administrators, as well as other stakeholders, must trust each other, and they need to give each other room to explore and make mistakes. Teachers and administrators must also extend that same trust to the students, especially when bringing about a change to personalized and digital learning. Educators must trust their students to utilize digital learning and technology to further their learning, while also building in expectations for proper technology use and safety policies.

In our work, we often see a principal, assistant principal, coach, or teacher who leads the discussion about the transition to digital learning with "Students will use the Internet inappropriately," "Students will lose their devices," or "Students will not be paying attention to the learning." Our experience with leaders who lead with these negative statements is that they will never be able to truly personalize learning. If you don't trust that students can learn to be responsible, can care about and be invested in their own learning, and can develop agency, then you should not try to move to personalized and digital learning. Students have always gone above and beyond what teachers have expected they could do. When students want to learn, when they are challenged to think and own their own learning, they will live up to and even exceed their potential. There will be those few students who fall short, but we cannot hold back the three hundred or five hundred or even two thousand students who are involved and committed because one student may make a poor choice. We cannot afford to distrust our students. They will sense it, and they will behave accordingly. If you have teachers who do not trust the students in your school, help them see what their students can do. Work with a teacher who sees the possibilities and then show the others. Work with student focus groups; provide examples of students (and not only the highflyers) succeeding. Process the outcomes of the teachers' own student-centered lessons.

Successful digital learning initiatives that truly change teaching and learning involve a culture of trust among administrators, teachers, students, and parents. Educators, in particular, must know that they have the opportunity to try new things and to learn from failures so that they can practice continuous improvement. The following key actions will support you as you examine, improve, and create an effective culture for the transition to personalized and digital learning:

- Address culture together.
- Model taking risks and making mistakes as part of the learning process.
- Inspect what you expect.

ADDRESS CULTURE TOGETHER

Troy shares that he struggled in his first year of moving to personalized learning because he did not stop and involve the teachers when he set out to determine institutional readiness. Part of building culture is listening to what people want and need and then deciding what they are ready to tackle. The idea of a shared vision and distributed leadership can affect culture. Troy describes an important example of how rushing ahead may have negatively affected the culture in his school:

> I have come to learn that institutional readiness is of utmost importance. I now use the term *institutional readiness* all the time. Your teachers need to be professionally developed in the areas of shift before communicating out to the community. When transitioning from a highly successful differentiated format at Hawk Ridge to more of an individualized (and later personalized) learning format, our public announcement was too early. While the district was branding a cohort of schools as Personalized Learning schools (my school a part of this), I was so impassioned by what I wanted our school to look like and do for kids that I went too bold too fast. I held town hall meetings with parents and answered questions very boldly—during the first week of school! I do believe we did deliver on what we said we would do for students within a personalized learning experience, but it came with a price. My amazing teachers got beat up pretty good by parents during the whole first quarter and especially at first quarter conferences. The teachers were growing in their understanding of how to implement learning paths and how to incorporate choice, but there was so much they were still not yet sure of. This contributed to some community unrest that did eventually settle down throughout the year as our processes and learning paths began to get really good and our vision for our individual students was realized.
>
> Now I am in a new environment as a school leader. Believe me, I think about institutional readiness in every decision I make. Do my teachers know what we are talking about within a particular shift? How much professional development can we do to promote understanding for our teachers before signing on to an actual implementation?

Troy's school culture was shaken and challenged by his choice to move forward before his teachers were ready. Ultimately, the school was able to make significant progress, which speaks to the culture that existed before the transition and the trust that the school community had for each other. Part of the work is to listen to teachers. Teachers, parents, students, and community members like to be asked for their input. Teachers are willing to work hard if their contributions are taken seriously. Asking the people who will be affected by the culture what they think begins to change how stakeholders view their school.

While principals play a big role in leading the establishment of an effective culture, you cannot do this work alone. One of the more inspiring examples we have seen of transitioning to an effective culture is in Talladega, Alabama. The systemic approach superintendent Suzanne Lacey took to this transition is admirable and worth looking at closely. The school system's approach to culture is almost unmatched. Visitors to Talladega are greeted with a positive energy, student leaders, empowered teachers, and principals and assistant principals who readily share the leadership of their school. The schools are positive learning environments, and students and teachers are eager to share. In one high school, in particular, only two or three years earlier, the opposite had been true. Teachers talked about how others harshly questioned why they would teach at the school, and they warily began working there hoping that the rumors they had heard about the negative culture of the school were not true. The principal and district instructional coach of this particular school chose to attack culture head-on. They recognized the problem and knew that to be able to accelerate the improvement of the culture, they could not undertake this task alone. The district coach and the principal declared Culture Days during the summer and invited the entire staff together to work on how they could improve their culture. The agendas for the days led with culture and required tough and in-depth discussions. The staff did not dance around the problems but instead created their own action steps—as a team. This method allowed them to take their shared vision and go a step further into a *shared approach to culture*.

Talladega's approach involved all stakeholders. They created a student advisory board to which students had to apply, but it was not just made up of a few select students who tended to be chosen for everything. Instead, this sizeable group became a part of the school's overarching vision, and the students themselves became the advocates and the messengers within and outside the school. Every student mattered. Special education students with significant needs started a coffee shop. They took orders from the adults in the building and provided specialized coffees to them. Doing this, the students learned math and language arts standards, while also focusing on the Four Cs. On our recent visit, members of the student advisory group shared their stories and took the lead in introducing us to the school. The school also adopted a professional dress code for students. In this high-need, low-socioeconomic school, having a dress code did not mean fancy clothes, but the students learned how to present themselves and took pride in doing so.

Talladega teachers not only addressed how they would be involved in the transition of the school culture but also had the flexibility to develop ideas in how to improve their student-centered PBL approach. Some courses involved local businesses such as a credit union; local business leaders became involved in teaching students important skills such as financial literacy, and they provided internships. Students began to see themselves in careers that they had not considered, which helped shift the culture to one of "I can."

Teachers were also integral to the professional learning of their colleagues, which contributed to distributed leadership, collaboration, and growth overall. A favorite quote from the district-level instructional coach Jennifer Barrett, who can be heard in a video from the visit, is: "People ask how we got the teachers on board. If they create it, there isn't a reason to get them on board."[3] During our visit to Talladega, three school board members wanted to talk with us. They, too, were part of the team working to impact the culture and the outcomes for students.

Talladega's approach was all-encompassing, but perhaps the most important lesson was that *the principal and the superintendent did not think that they could or should address culture alone.* Having the team of teachers work to identify the problems, create the plan, and implement the solutions changed the culture before the first step was ever taken in the school itself. You could, and arguably should, also invite students to be a part of the discussion, planning, and implementation.

MODEL TAKING RISKS AND MAKING MISTAKES

An important strategy for building a culture in which teachers and students can take risks and try new things is to model that action. If you, as the principal and lead learner, are willing to try something new and then fail—and even better, do it in front of teachers or students—you create a safe place in which students and teachers can and should do the same thing. To do this, you must push yourself outside your comfort zone. There are many different ways of doing this. You could try using a new tool during a faculty meeting. Your effort may go as planned, but it might not. If it does not work smoothly, stop and acknowledge the failure by saying, "I realize that this is how you must feel when you implement your lesson plan and something does not go right." Ask the faculty to help you solve the problem and demonstrate your willingness to use a different approach on the fly.

Drew Ware, a principal in Chapel Hill, North Carolina, begins faculty meetings by celebrating failure. He asks each staff member to reflect on something that they tried with their lessons that didn't work out as planned and what they learned from the experience or how would they do it differently next time. After a brief reflection, teachers are asked to share with a colleague. At one point, they even had a "faffle"—a raffle drawn from failures and mistakes that teachers had happen and then entered into a drawing. While this drawing was a fun and silly way to acknowledge failures, Ware was actually celebrating trying—trying new things and being willing to take a risk. By asking teachers to reflect on things that didn't go as planned, Ware acknowledged the teachers' need to fail forward and learn from their mistakes.

Morris Grove Elementary School principal Amy Rickard shares the potential danger of too much collaboration in limiting risk taking. She has found that, at times, the professional learning community (PLC) model may actually become so collaborative—with deep trusts and a shared ownership of students—that no one teacher wants to step out, take risks, and act alone. As a basis of trust, the PLC can go a long way, but as a leader, you may need to push certain individuals to take the risk and lead. In this case, Amy often has an instructional technology facilitator or another coach or leader who knows the teachers well to support a teacher in taking the step:

> One of the leaders may nudge someone because she knows which teachers are willing to take risks. So, she can say, "Let's try this and let's see." It may fail, and they are okay with that. Have a good support person who has your back create a safe place to try new things and have that person learning alongside them.

Another way to model taking risks is being willing to ask for help and being willing to declare that you do not know all the answers. When John Bernia, former principal of Carleton Middle School, saw a significant challenge or realized a big problem as he reviewed data or got feedback, he knew that he could do a better job of tackling this issue by asking others to help him figure it out. He models that it is acceptable and even encouraged to ask for input and ideas to solve the problem:

> I'm known for something I call the "Big Think." I invite staff to stay after work for an hour to talk about a big idea. I start by framing the problem or issue; then I sit, listen, and take notes. After analyzing my notes, I put into action what I heard.

At my last school, we had a "Big Think" about technology integration. Those who stayed were teachers who were exploring different tools in their practice. After our meeting, they became "our tech team." Using my substitute teacher budget, I paid for release time for them to survey staff and plan differentiated professional development for our teachers. We used staff meeting time, conference periods, and additional substitute teacher dollars to provide training for teachers. When a staff member tried something in their classroom, the "trainers" were in our school, so they had built-in people to ask follow-up questions or talk about how things went. Our culture became "professional development by our teachers, for our teachers," and it made trying something new a safe idea. My role, aside from financing and creating the time, was to follow up and ask how things were going, continuously reflecting and evaluating how this was working for all of our teachers.

The "Big Think" happens when you throw out the big problems and give a framework to solve the problem and figure out what we can do. It's a think about what's possible. Any employee can come. People are motivated when they have control. We've given them autonomy.

Being willing to ask for help, being willing to take risks, and being willing to make mistakes are invaluable in creating a culture that is effective for something as systemic and big as a transition to personalized and digital learning.

INSPECT WHAT YOU EXPECT

At the beginning of the chapter, we cautioned against sending mixed messages to teachers about the shared vision and what is really expected each day. Some of these crossed signals are caused by moving toward a new vision for personalized and digital learning without giving up anything else. Teachers are resistant to new initiatives because they often see them as yet another fad, something transitory with no hope of gaining traction. While teachers will likely try to comply, helping them see that a shift to personalized and digital learning is not a fad may not be easy. Knowing that personalized and digital learning is about the heart of teaching and learning itself, however, you can help build and sustain an effective culture by being consistent with your focus and what you expect in your daily interactions with teachers, students, and other stakeholders.

One tangible area that can confuse teachers and lead to unrest and a less trusting culture is evaluation and feedback. If teachers are taking risks and trying new things but feel as though feedback or interactions during walk-throughs are not focused on the shared vision of the school or understanding of mistakes, they will not feel confident in their work. Mary Ann still remembers the humiliation caused by one such principal visit eighteen years ago. She had gone out on a limb to utilize a new technology. All the students in her class were raising their hands, eager to answer a question about marine biology. Rather than engage with the big picture, the principal went over to a shy student who, in a rare moment of connectedness, had raised his hand. The principal didn't encourage him but instead took off his hat and reminded him that students do not wear hats inside the classroom. That little boy was crushed, and Mary Ann, as his teacher, was, too. She had been focusing on creating student-centered lessons in which students could learn the standards in a high-need school, but the principal's message was in direct conflict with what Mary Ann viewed as important. The informal interactions can be constructive—and even more important—can help support the building of an effective culture.

Evaluations and informal walk-throughs are opportunities to show consistency of that shared vision, provide constructive feedback, and reinforce what is important in your school for students every day. Most principals strive to walk through classrooms in their school informally each week or even each day. This practice can correspond to the "Gotcha!" mentality if the only feedback given is negative or about themes that do not support the school vision.

Many principals go a step further to reinforce what matters through informal visits. Michael created a simple walk-through instrument that provided immediate feedback on student engagement, an area in which his school was focused. He would walk through the classrooms in his typical visits and then complete a Google form with one question about student engagement that he immediately shared with the teacher. The topic was consistent with the school's focus on student learning, and the approach was transparent. Michael was also willing and available to discuss what he saw or ideas for improvement, but he was careful to ensure that the feedback was never seen as punitive:

> I believe so much in the power of walk-throughs. I think they should always be announced because I am measuring "What do people know how to do?" When I am doing those walk-throughs, instead of having fifteen things I am looking for, I look for one thing, like student engagement. Then the conversation becomes, "They are engaged because. . . ." The teachers knew my

patterns when I walked every morning and knew the walks were for relationships. I high-fived and danced outside the door. These were all relationship building. We spend so much time checking off a box when we should be building relationships with people.

While at Hawk Ridge Elementary, Troy took the idea of having a presence in the school to a whole new level. He decided to give up his office to free up space, but also to ensure that he spent considerable time in classrooms and in collaborative spaces throughout the school. He wanted teachers and students to feel comfortable with him in their classrooms, and he also wanted to spend enough time in classrooms to understand how the transition to personalized learning was working on a regular basis. Troy would sometimes take his laptop and sit in the back of a room for two hours at a time. He would be working on his computer while also taking in what was happening with the teachers and students. Teachers at Hawk Ridge were very comfortable talking about the challenges of team teaching and moving to personalized pathways in front of Troy. They were willing to share what worked. This evidence of a culture of trust in which teachers could talk about what worked well and what did not work well provided an important basis for the transition. People made mistakes and encountered hurdles, but they had the space to talk about them with each other and with Troy to figure out how to support their students and the transition to personalized learning.

As you place an emphasis on the area that is important to you, you also should be willing to work with teachers who need assistance. Regardless of the types of efforts in a school, the mean years of teaching experience, or even the continuity of staff, teachers will always be at different places in terms of readiness or willingness for growth in certain areas. Tim Lauer, former principal of Meriwether Lewis Elementary School, sometimes played matchmaker to help those who were more comfortable with teachers who may need more help:

> I think for some of our teachers, incorporating technology is harder for them because they didn't grow up with it, or they are just less comfortable with it. I've said, "Let's sit down and plan and talk about how you might use some tools in your classroom." Or, I work across grade-level teams where I play matchmaker. For example, Mark wants to do this project. I'll ask a more hesitant teacher, "Would you like your classroom to be involved with that?" You have to evangelize a little bit. You have to do some professional development with

them. They need to know to use the technology not because it's cool, but because it can enhance what kids take away, enhance a deeper learning.

Throughout the course of the school week, I'm in every classroom at least twice. I start the day with the older grades and then pop in and just check in with teachers. I pick up laptops. I spend extended periods of time in classrooms or parts of the buildings. Doing this affords me interactions with teachers and students. The interactions can be in a classroom or near a music room. I don't have to be in my office to do what I need to do.

I provide a lot of informal feedback. There might be something that I follow up with in an e-mail, but I have more casual interactions while they are working. I might ask a question about the activity, or they might mention something. I have played with various tools for feedback, but I have found that the conversations—and a thank you when I leave—[let] them know I'm not there to evaluate or judge. The evaluation is cumulative.

These examples show different ways for you to be consistent and transparent about what is important to you and the school's vision. Teachers will appreciate understanding what is expected, and you can also use this approach as a way to have ongoing conversations about how they can improve. As you build a culture by addressing culture together, modeling, and inspecting what you expect, you will also want to make sure that you celebrate and regularly discuss what is important.

Michael's approach to celebrations and communication was to use "hallway huddles." Picture music, cheering, and focused discussion.

The hallway huddles have two parts. The first one is to celebrate what's happened in the last week, instead of waiting. People need words of affirmation. We did a book study with *The Five Languages of Appreciation in the Workplace* by Gary Chapman and Paul White (Northfield Publishing, Chicago: 2011) and found teachers need affirmation. Doing that every Friday was huge. The second thing was to clarify. I sent one e-mail to my staff each week—every Thursday—with all of the expectations after celebrations in the hallway huddle. I would ask for any clarification. Once the momentum was going, others could lead the discussion through the questions.

TRY IT TOMORROW

Building community and an environment of collaboration is an integral component of an effective culture and essential as you transition to digital learning. Providing opportunities for teachers to work together in fun ways is an important piece in building this culture that should be done throughout the year.

1. **Use a tool like GooseChase to set up scavenger hunts for your staff.**[4] Have teachers work in teams (which might be a good opportunity to strategically assign them to groups that they don't always work with) to complete the missions in a given time frame. The missions can be related to school activities or support school pride or could be just fun. After the scavenger hunt is finished, take the time to debrief with your staff using these possible questions: What did you learn about someone else on your team that you didn't know? What did you learn about yourself as a learner during this activity? How might you use something like this with your students?

    Check out Common Sense Media, which has written help for teachers using this technique with students, if you want to learn more.[5]

2. **BreakoutEDU is a great way to build collaboration among your staff,** especially when you follow up the challenge with a debriefing conversation that includes questions like these: How did each team member contribute to the success of the team? What did you learn about a team member during this process that you didn't already know?

    BreakoutEDU games give teams a series of challenges that must be solved in a specified amount of time to solve a mystery. Modeled after escape rooms, BreakoutEDU games are fun for adults and give them some ideas for how they might use these games in their own classrooms. Visit the website for more information and to see games that educators have created.[6]

5

Develop Professional Learning That Is Personalized and Job-Embedded

You have to differentiate. We know when we teach kids, we have to differentiate, but we need to create options for teachers, options that are about how people participate and the topics they are learning.

—MICHAEL ARMSTRONG

Think of your most effective professional learning experience. Really pause for a minute and identify a specific learning opportunity that you were engaged in that made a significant difference to you professionally. Was it a particular cohort that you worked with over time? Was it an intense two-day experience in which you had to work to develop a plan or solution? Was it an awesome class or membership organization that contributed to your growth?

When you think about your particular experience, what qualities or characteristics emerge? What made the experience meaningful to you? In asking hundreds of school and district leaders, coaches, and teachers this same question, we have found anecdotally that the most effective learning opportunities typically validate what research tells us about effective professional learning. Research emphasizes that effective professional learning must do the following:

- be intensive, ongoing, and connected to practice
- focus on student learning and address the teaching of specific curriculum content
- align with school improvement priorities and goals
- build strong working relationships among teachers[1]

While these characteristics might seem rather obvious, it is surprising how many professional learning opportunities continue to fall into the traditional two-hour workshop mode. Teachers gather in a meeting room or the cafeteria, and someone comes in and talks at them for the better part of two hours. The focus of these sessions is on imparting information, and once that's done, the workshop is over. At best, teachers will engage in the workshop session itself for two hours and then leave, alone, with new information, excited to try new things in their classrooms. Often, however, weeks go by and teachers realize they have not changed anything in their instruction, in their classroom, or in their thinking. For a teacher working alone, the process of taking information from a workshop and working it into the classroom can be very difficult. Why, then, is the two-hour workshop mode still the go-to professional learning mode of choice? While most principals understand the importance of professional learning, how you and other school leaders implement and guide professional learning can make or break any effort to improve instruction or transition to personalized or digital learning. It's time to start looking outside the two-hour workshop box for professional development opportunities.

To start thinking about professional development differently, look at all the types of professional learning options that are available. Examine how you dedicate time, coaching, and modeling; then begin personalizing your professional learning options based on needs of the teachers.

It has traditionally been difficult for districts and schools to provide access to meaningful professional learning opportunities. It's important to provide opportunities that align with the vision your school as created. In a 2009 National Staff Development Council study, "nearly half of all U.S. teachers are dissatisfied with their opportunities for professional development." Personalizing staff development opportunities will increase teacher satisfaction as well as provide real opportunities for growth.[2]

Sometimes, your role may need to be that of the matchmaker. Getting to know your teachers and their strengths and weaknesses is crucial to this process. Based on what you know about your staff, you can then offer pointed information to help educators see how they might connect or learn from each other. This is a key strategy in a classroom, and it works just as well with educators and other stakeholders. Tim Lauer, former principal of Meriwether Lewis Elementary School, shares how he connected teachers to resources and to each other:

> I think what I try to do for teachers is thinking of what they are currently doing and knowing what is coming up. This provides me with an opportunity to find and research things. For example, fourth-grade teachers. Our fourth-grade history used to [focus on] the Oregon Trail. I've been encouraging teachers to look a little bit more to broaden that lens and talk more about indigenous people who were here and other groups that came to Oregon. I find my role is to find the resources that a particular teacher needs to improve or enhance their curriculum. I try to differentiate PD for what teachers need rather than assume one size fits all. When I have staff that knows something or has a strength, I point teachers to them for support. Another aspect is Twitter. Twitter has been a powerful tool for teachers who are looking to connect with others.

As a principal, you have an opportunity to create and encourage professional learning opportunities that are highly effective and also personalized to meet the needs of each teacher. Like our students, each teacher has different strengths, challenges, interests, and needs, and they do change over time. Some full-staff sessions in which everyone is learning together can be important, but it is also essential that teachers are able to work on and develop the skills they need to be more effective. Thinking about each teacher as a learner—each with certain strengths, challenges, and needs—can help you maximize the potential of professional learning to build capacity among your teachers and improve instruction and student outcomes in your school.

Michael Armstrong, former principal of Bugg Creative Arts Magnet School, reminds us:

> You have to differentiate. We know when we teach kids, we need to differentiate, but we need to create options from PLCs, options that are about how people participate and what they use. "Stealing awesome" is creating a culture where people are learning from each other. This includes less philosophy and more action. So many times, we knew by October what was not working, but we already had a schedule and we had to wait until the next summer to change it. If something is not working, start new. We need to be fluid—like with kids.

Part of building an effective culture is placing an emphasis on professional learning in an ongoing rather than incidental way. Just as learning doesn't stop for our students, our own learning and development don't just stop until we have time to fit them in. Our own learning needs to become an integral part of our identity as educators. As educators, we need to think of ourselves not only as people who have some of the answers but also as people who have a lot of the questions. Professional development needs to be a purposeful, intentional goal of teachers and principals. And it must be obvious to everyone that this is going on.

Professional learning opportunities that are job-embedded, ongoing, and relevant to an educator's context are absolutely critical for the transition to personalized and digital learning. Utilizing coaches to model and coteach, valuing informal professional development, using faculty meetings as learning opportunities, and having teachers lead professional learning in the school are all strategies to build successful and meaningful opportunities for educators. The following areas offer ways to strengthen professional learning and changes in teacher practice:

- Make time for professional learning.
- Ensure coaching and mentoring are available and supported.
- Take advantage of peer-to-peer opportunities (observations, learning walks, and site visits) as a means to professional learning.
- Encourage and honor informal and formal professional learning.

MAKE TIME FOR PROFESSIONAL LEARNING

When you ask teachers about the roadblocks or hurdles to transitioning to personalized learning, the most common reason for not making the transition is a lack of time. Teachers are busy. In her own research, Mary Ann found that teachers need almost forty-eight minutes for planning and grading for every hour of instruction.[3] This amount of time is not surprising when you think about what it takes to plan carefully and provide constructive feedback, and when you think of the realities of time, you can quickly see that teachers are always left needing more time. More often than not, teachers will finish everything they possibly can for kids even if it means not prioritizing their own professional learning. You can help teachers make professional learning a priority by creating time, emphasizing job-embedded options, and modeling the importance of taking time.

Teachers who are committed to their own learning understand that taking the time makes them better at what they do every day, and that, in turn, helps students learn and grow. Principals who are able to make time for professional learning and development do not have more hours in a day, but they do use them differently. As you work to create the vision for personalized and digital learning for your school, you may feel torn between balancing professional learning that everyone needs to participate in and what development could be based more on individual needs. Troy Moore, former principal of Hawk Ridge Elementary School, shares how he balanced schoolwide and personalized professional learning:

> I believe the best professional development is a combination of Unifying PD and Personalized PD. Unifying PD are those strategies or implementations that you want everyone to begin work on, and it is important that a common language is developed. This requires most of the teaching staff to be involved. The importance here is that the training is relevant to all in attendance. Overview of shifts within the core subjects can be done within the whole group, but the deep dives in these PDs should be sectioned out into age/grade appropriateness.
>
> Personalized PD is developing the process for passions to be infused in the PD process. For instance, for next year I am developing a pathway format for staff to choose from a menu of deep dives that they want to move forward in instructionally (choice of one per semester) and a passion-based opportunity that is personally enriching and possibly community building (for example, sewing, app development, etc.).

Michael created professional development Mondays when his dean of professional learning was available and ran interactive, hands-on sessions all day every Monday. Teachers' schedules provided longer blocks of time by having back-to-back specials or specials next to lunchtime, which freed them up to participate in a less-hurried manner. Michael even created an additional "specials" class with blocks for science lab to free up more of teachers' time by tapping into a skill set of one or two of his teachers. These sessions were not structured as "sit and get," but rather teachers explored and played with technology tools and resources, or they created lessons together with the dean of professional learning there to guide them. Once the longer blocks are established through some creative scheduling, teachers can also engage in informal professional learning through Twitter or Edmodo, or they can have the opportunity to seek out just-in-time learning to answer a specific question. These shorter learning opportunities can support the longer, more intensive experiences.

Faculty meetings have traditionally been used to update teachers on the things they need to know about what's coming up. Updates can take different forms such as e-mail or website updates. You can flip your faculty meetings—and flip your teachers' learning—by having teachers watch a video ahead of time and then discuss guided questions at the meetings. This video should be related to your shared vision and/or emphasize a specific area in which you need to focus. You could ask a teacher that you saw facilitating an effective lesson to lead the faculty through the meeting. Having teachers facilitate opens up the meetings and shares ownership. Faculty meetings then shift from top-down lectures to shared learning opportunities. You can have teachers participate in a design challenge such as creating a flying saucer using circuits. These opportunities can help your teachers think differently about problem solving and learner agency. You can design learning activities that are fun but, more importantly, model teaching and learning (and point out how you developed them or where you learned them). You can model design thinking or even the importance of coding by having teachers engage in contests with Spheros (small robots controlled by relatively simple coding apps). Finally, working collaboratively to solve problems or discuss issues or events can also help make your culture more effective. If your teachers and staff learn and try new ideas together, they will also be more likely to connect in their day-to-day work when they have a question or want to solve a challenge.

Principal Alison Hramiec of the Boston Day and Evening Academy identifies an instructional focus each year and then develops job-embedded professional learning to support that goal. She explains her process and shows the check-in, the identification of specific needs by team, and also the opportunity to implement and reflect:

> Professional learning and growth is a process at BDEA that is incremental. We start each year identifying the student and professional learning goal for the school year. This will be one overarching but specific instructional goal to which each teacher will align his or her individual goal. Our instructional leadership team (ILT) generates the whole-school instructional focus. They

review last year's goal, review data (staff surveys that assess progress on last year's goal and student academic performance data) and any outside accountability measures we must address. Through this process, we prioritize our student learning and instructional goal for the coming school year.

For example, this year our instructional goal was focused on having all teachers develop cognitively demanding tasks/lessons (CDTs) in all of their classrooms. We had spent the last three years working on making sure our assessments were rigorous, so this was a natural next step. To support teachers' achievement of this goal, our lead teachers conducted a whole-school PD workshop that helped us all gain a common understanding of what it meant to design and facilitate CDT. The lead teachers shared research as well as materials they had gathered from our districtwide PD a few weeks earlier. They modeled best practices for teaching a CDT as they presented the materials, and they provided time for teachers to reflect and think about the application of this new knowledge in their classroom.

Once all teachers had a common understanding of the whole-school instructional goal, they met in departments to shape the goal specific to their department's work. Math, for example, wanted to spend time as a department sharing and learning how to craft math lessons that asked students to solve open-ended math problems that had multiple solutions. How would they, as instructors, provide just the right amount of scaffolding so that the math problem was cognitively demanding for all students? What were some techniques they could share that would support struggling students? The Humanities department, on the other hand, created a goal that focused on students' reading skills. They wanted to continue their work understanding and scaffolding the text they were using in their classrooms so that students were being exposed to increased text complexity and decreased scaffold supports.

During instructional leadership team (ILT) meetings, department leaders and lead teachers created common tools (a rubric for assessing CDT) and protocols (for looking at teacher lessons) that each department could use in their department time throughout the year. We practiced using the tools as a small group, making adjustments to them, so that when leaders left and used the tools in their department meetings, we were all consistent with language and student learning expectations. Many of the tools we create are simplified versions of the many tools already made available online, modified to support our instructional goal focus.

As a school community, we value the expertise within the building. My role as a school leader is to continue to identify and highlight the best practices I see as I visit classrooms. Often times at our weekly staff meetings, staff will be asked to share a quick practice that was successful in their classroom.

This could be a classroom management technique, a tool that helped students utilize their habits of mind or success, etc. I have found that when we use the resources inside our school, the examples are meaningful and relevant to our work. As a leader, in the same way we ask students to own their learning, I am asking teachers to own their professional growth.

Helping teachers identify the area of focus, aligned to the school's vision and goals, while also allowing for teams and individuals to determine their own goals creates ownership from the beginning. Alison also showed that professional learning is a priority by making the focus cohesive, while dedicating the time for teachers to learn as a staff, as a team, and as individuals. Teachers want their professional learning to connect to their practice and be relevant for what they are doing tomorrow.

For teachers to do this well, they must work with their team, or other teachers on their grade level, to plan lessons that both meet the standards and engage all learners. This collaboration takes time and requires a culture of trust among the team. School leaders must first recognize the need for teachers to work together in their lesson design and then encourage and empower teachers to take on this role. Curriculum coaches can play an important role in this process as they help guide teachers in designing their lessons that meet the standards.

ENSURE COACHING AND MENTORING ARE AVAILABLE AND SUPPORTED

Research shows the importance of coaching or mentoring in translating professional development and personal mastery into changes in classroom practice. Figure 5.1 demonstrates research by Joyce and Showers that reminds us of the importance of building in these supports for teachers. It is when coaching and mentoring are combined with other learning experiences that changes in the classroom increase dramatically. We can put a great deal of emphasis on learning, on workshops, even on attending conferences or other opportunities, but until teachers work with a coach or mentor in person (or virtually), you are unlikely to see meaningful shifts in their work with students.

As you reflect on the importance of coaching and mentoring, you may immediately think about certain people in your building who are tasked with this role officially, or you may be thinking that you don't have anyone with this role. Some schools have library media specialists, instructional or cur-

Figure 5.1 Importance of coaching and mentoring

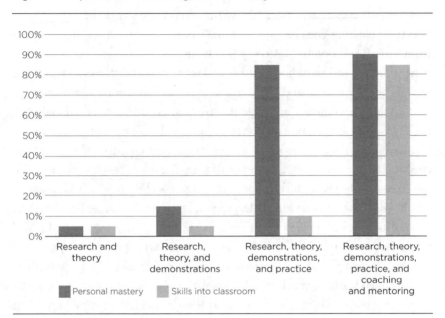

Chart created from research by Bruce Joyce and Beverly Showers, *Student Achievement Through Staff Development,* 3rd ed. (Alexandria, VA: Association for Supervision and Curriculum Development, 2002).

riculum coaches, instructional technology facilitators, literacy coaches, math coaches, or instructional resource teachers. Others have grade-level coaches or district-based content area coaches that work across schools. Regardless of the titles your school has, you should consider three important questions:

- Are these individuals actually spending their time planning, researching, coteaching, and offering feedback to teachers?
- Is the coaching aligned to your vision for teaching and learning, or is the coaching disparate and possibly contradictory?
- Can other individuals, including possibly yourself, spend time coaching teachers?

The reason that coaching and mentoring are so important is that they provide encouragement and accountability to try new things. More importantly, coaches and mentors provide the thoughtful scaffolding to help teachers learn and grow, even if they are afraid of making a mistake or of something not working. In an effective culture, being vulnerable while working with coaches becomes much more likely. Research shows that the influence of effective coaching goes beyond a teacher's practice to students, the teacher's team, and the school itself. A coach determines where the teacher is in terms of her practice and her school setting, and using his expertise, is able to guide the teacher to make changes. A coach acts as a collaborator and a support.[4]

Coaching and mentoring can come from many different individuals, but the key is that coaches have dedicated professional time built into their schedule; have opportunities to grow and learn in their coaching skills; and are encouraged to work across a subset of all teachers, not only with the ones who are comfortable asking for support. Although coaches may or may not have official coaching or mentoring titles, several key roles, including library media specialists and content area specialists, may be able to increase job-embedded professional learning by providing time and supporting relationships.

One challenge that often emerges with instructional technology facilitators, blended learning coaches, or others with *technology* or *digital* in their title is that they can easily become the go-to-person for fixing technology when something doesn't work. This is especially true if the school and/or district does not have adequate technicians. Principals play a big role in ensuring that this is not the case because these roles should be instructional ones, with separate roles for the technicians. You must also empower these individuals to say no to fixing things so that they can do their job.

Library Media Specialists

One of the most untapped and potentially effective coaching resources is the library media specialist (or librarian, or media coordinator). When we look across schools that are effectively transitioning to personalized and digital learning, we see that most of them view the library media specialist as an integral part of their coaching support and leadership team. Library media specialists can coplan and coimplement lessons with teachers. For example, a project-based learning (PBL) lesson that requires students to drive their research and content creation would likely be strengthened with the help of a library media specialist.

Library media specialists also have the opportunity to coach teachers and students by demonstrating what learner agency can look like because of the way they arrange their space. Few others have the opportunity to redesign a significant learning space; but in doing so, library media specialists can model what is possible for students. For example, the media center can become a maker space for students to use during flexible time, and this is not limited to having materials for physical building or design. If the media center has GarageBand or other music-making applications, a 3-D printer, a green screen, and perhaps design software, students can explore and try new ideas aligned to their interests or curiosities. If a school moves to a Genius Hour or 20% Time for students, the library media center can become a central place for discovery, trial-and-error, and production. The media specialist can become a mentor to both students and teachers, offering up new ideas, new technologies, and the space to experiment and collaborate.

Content Area or Curriculum Coaches

Many districts across the country have moved toward having literacy, math, or other content area coaches. In some districts, especially at the high school level, content chairs in a high school can mentor others in the department because of their deep subject knowledge. One role that these coaches have is to provide ongoing, embedded professional development. Content coaches should maintain an encouraging demeanor and act in a nonevaluative and nonpunitive manner. These coaches help establish the distributed leadership model in schools and encourage a collaborative culture in which failure is, in fact, an option. It is also important to realize that content and curriculum area coaches can not only advise and collaborate on content-specific knowledge and practices but can also push and guide teachers toward personalizing learning and utilizing digital content and resources.

Coaching Skills and Adult Learning

Many coaches are tapped for their coaching roles because of the excellent work they do in their classrooms. However, just because someone is an excellent teacher of children does not necessarily mean that person is prepared or has the skill set to teach or coach adults. You can help coaches by ensuring that they are involved in professional learning themselves and giving them time to work with other coaches, possibly from other schools, to share approaches and strategies. You also should ensure that you and your coaches have a shared vision for their role and that they have opportunities to learn about adult learning theory.

Beyond encouraging coaches to seek out professional learning, you can guide them to develop a coaching action plan. Many effective approaches can be applied to coaching, and each coach might choose a different approach or strategy. These strategies might differ with each teacher a coach works with. Work with your coaches to ensure they have a plan that ensures all teachers will eventually participate in coaching and encourage each coach to have a systematic plan for how to meet the needs of teachers.

TAKE ADVANTAGE OF PEER-TO-PEER OPPORTUNITIES AS A MEANS TO PROFESSIONAL LEARNING

In addition to being coaches or mentors, many opportunities exist for teachers to support one another's growth. As obvious as this is, it is often one of the most underutilized strategies for professional development in schools. Teachers rarely take the time to observe one another in their classrooms. "At least 90 percent of teachers in the U.S. have participated in professional development that involves workshops or short-term conferences, and only 22 percent have observed classrooms in another school."[5] Support your teachers in their efforts to find time to do this during the school day. Make it a priority for them because observation can be transformative. Teachers begin to see each other as experts and colleagues in positive ways. They begin to rely on each other as supports for what they're doing in their own classrooms. Observing, asking questions of, and learning with and from other teachers are incredibly powerful tools for professional learning.

Building the culture of trust and using coaches as supports, Principal Amy Rickard has instituted ways for teachers to observe and provide feedback to one another at Morris Grove Elementary School, taking peer-to-peer professional learning to a new level:

> One thing that we started last year, which has now come full circle, is coaching labs in literacy. The literacy coaches do content-focused coaching and video the teachers. Then the teachers watch [the videos] in the PLCs. They are helping teachers work through the video, and then teachers use the observation protocol from IFL [Institute for Learning] to talk about and reflect on the process. They follow a peer feedback cycle, and then the team highlights the next steps. This is highly intensive, and they couldn't do it without the

coaches; but it's really raised the level of trust. They used to do peer observations. This is not taking away from instruction, but it creates an opportunity to say, "Here is a problem of practice; help me." Then the grade level says, "We want to focus on this," i.e., small group instruction. This is very specific to PLCs.

Michael instituted Learning Walks, or Walking PLC, an approach that has been used in many schools across the country. This activity involves having a group of teachers visit classrooms in their building with the plan of then discussing the instruction they see. Sometimes this discussion may focus on a particular aspect of the school's vision, such as collaboration, learning environment, or learner agency; and other times it may be a more general discussion based on what teachers observe. Learning walks may be used as a way to build an effective culture, but they also require some important ground rules so that they are viewed as positive learning tools rather than punitive or evaluative. It is typically helpful to have a coach or a teacher leader lead the walks, and you may want to ask some of your teachers who are the most comfortable with the process to be the ones visited in the beginning. Eventually, every classroom can be involved, but you can start slowly and also help teachers see something you want them to learn and discuss. For example, if one teacher is especially strong at utilizing a collaborative digital tool to have students work together to create products related to a question that strongly supports the standards, you could ask to visit during that time. If you are hoping that teachers can see how changing the classroom setup and moving away from desks in rows, especially in middle or high school, can support changes in teaching and learning, you may want to visit a teacher who has made such changes to furniture arrangement or room organization. When you leave these rooms, you should stop to discuss the particular area—whether collaboration (and how digital tools may support that) or learning environments. This is a safe place for teachers to ask questions and also to share what they noticed. They can hear from one another so that this technique becomes a relevant, tangible, professional learning experience, especially if they start brainstorming how they might integrate some of the strategies in their own classrooms.

Superintendent Suzanne Lacey in Talladega, Alabama, has provided a leadership role for teachers through the "Experts Down the Hall" initiative instituted throughout her district to support each other in the use of digital learning:

We have a specialized teacher-leader network that works on the integration of technology. We have a couple of administrators and a tech coordinator, [whom] they work with exclusively. They grow and rotate every year, and part of their work is identifying "Experts Down the Hall," and teachers now have that distinction. If you are working on a particular skill, hopefully the "Expert Down the Hall" will be there if you need it. The teachers who lead this group may change, but the core base are the digital learning specialists. It is fun that stars emerge, and no one knew them; but they discovered their niche. The collective work is so important to everything that we do because we value and appreciate the greatness of our teachers. We couldn't do this without them—it would be impossible.

"Experts Down the Hall" helps teachers know whom to ask when they have a question or want to brainstorm ideas, and it also allows a newer teacher or perhaps one who has not been recognized to have a mentor role for others. One of the great benefits of a program like "Experts Down the Hall" is the development of distributed leadership and the trust it engenders among your faculty. They begin to trust and to rely on each other.

Suzanne Lacey and Derek McCoy, who is principal of West Rowan Middle School, both talk extensively about the importance of showing and not just talking about what is possible in utilizing coaches by taking coaches and teachers (and additional stakeholders that would benefit) to visit other schools and districts. Even as Suzanne and Talladega schools have achieved great success, with a 94 percent graduation rate in 2015, they know that they need to continue to learn and grow to meet the needs of their students. The learning does not stop. Other schools and other districts are always testing and utilizing new ideas, so learning from their successes and failures is beneficial. As Suzanne says,

> I think, as a leader, it's always important to find what other districts are doing well and learn from them. We are in an unlikely place to reach out to the world. We are a high-poverty, rural community. But we are going to do our dead-level best to search and research greatness—and find a way to learn from these people. Seeing is believing to help people catch the vision. We became a member of the League of Innovative Schools. This has been an answer to this next stage of what we hope will be phenomenal work. You need to associate yourself with good people and districts that are doing well and providing great work for their kids. You need to do some research and study that. Being a member of the League will help supplement what we are doing and give us

that broader vision. We have to want more and learn from others! The greatest thing has been the learning and networking from other districts doing things well. We learn all of the time.

ENCOURAGE AND HONOR INFORMAL AND FORMAL PROFESSIONAL LEARNING

Like students, teachers learn in many different ways. Some of the paths that learning takes are planned and carefully structured. Other learning paths might be less formal. As the principal, you have a chance to model and to encourage both formal and informal professional learning in and beyond what is provided through the school district. You also play an important role in helping teachers understand in what areas they may need additional professional learning or certain opportunities that may inspire them or continue to help them develop their own practice.

Teachers often know where they need or want professional learning when you ask them and start talking to them about possibilities, but they may not arrive at the ideas or priorities on their own. Teachers may also feel limited by time, resources, or funding to participate in professional learning. Informal professional learning can play a significant role in developing teachers' agency for their own learning, while also more reasonably fitting into their lives. For a long time, informal professional development consisted of conversations in the hallway or ideas pulled from the *Mailbox* magazine that teachers received once a month. Digital technology has changed all of that. Digital content is instantly available. Websites provide lesson plans, resources, and suggestions by grade level and class. Teachers can follow Twitter hashtags. Edcamps and other opportunities to build professional learning networks (PLNs) have dramatically expanded the possibilities for teachers. Helping teachers find and utilize those resources is not only important but also necessary. Showing teachers that you value their informal learning encourages them to continue to spend their time searching out new learning opportunities.

Edcamps

Edcamps are something akin to unconferences or user-created meetups in which those attending determine the topics and drive the content themselves.[6] Some Edcamps are simply dictated by location (Edcamp Beach or Edcamp Chicago), whereas others have a more general focus, such as Edcamp for

Leaders. These conferences are overall low stress and low cost; plus they provide a flexible and safe place for educators to come together, identify common issues and concerns, and then choose how they want to spend their time. Although these sessions are very discussion and sharing based, the discussions do not necessarily begin and end on the meeting day itself. Educators tend to grow their PLNs to include members of these Edcamps, and often members will continue to communicate through Voxer (an audio-message-based app), Twitter, Edmodo, or even through e-mail. Some schools are beginning to hold their own Edcamps, or you could consider partnering with other elementary, middle, or high schools in your district. Edcamps can be content area specific. Math teachers may naturally gravitate toward one another, especially if they are struggling with new standards, content, or assessment. A topic may emerge around digital learning or alternative assessments. Edcamps can also be technology specific, centered on learning how to use a specific tool across disciplines. Edcamps are the ultimate example of voice and choice, and they model student-centered learning for teachers.

Social Media

Social media is not simply a hobby or something you engage in while waiting in line. For many, social media has become a gateway to learning and connecting with others. As a school leader, you can show the power of social media connections by highlighting what you learn or sharing your connections through your own PLN.

In his role as principal of Meriwether Lewis Elementary School, Tim worked to get people on his team who were all working toward the same vision. He also tried to help educators build their own networks within the school and nationally or internationally. Tim modeled how Twitter, in particular, allowed him to expand his PLN to encompass a group of leaders across the country that he relied on and communicated with regularly. He even got to meet some of them in person at conferences or other convenings. About that time, he says,

> We brought on four staff in the last three to four years. Separately, they're great teachers and people, but in addition, they're great at collaborating and sharing their work. We've gotten to a point where we have nineteen teachers sharing on Twitter every day. What that does is not only point out something

about Mr. Hanson's math activity, but also that another teacher saw that, which leads to further conversation and a whole level of engagement that would be there just like walking down the hall and saying hi to each other. It's tough when you're isolated in your room. With getting the right people on board (using Twitter), you have a whole mix of people talking. Those teachers who might wait and hold back now have someone to show them the way. This year, things have gotten real traction, and tech has been key.

Social media provides the power to share the great things that are happening. However, another benefit of sharing what a teacher is doing or a lesson in which students are engaged is that it highlights instruction and pedagogy and ways that teachers are making progress toward your shared vision. Within your school, teachers can learn and get ideas from each other; and outside of your school, teachers can start to see what is happening in other places and expand their PLN.

Microcredentials

Microcredentials, sometimes referred to as digital badges, represent the achievement or attainment of a skill or knowledge base. They are competency based in that you must demonstrate that you have learned and/or applied something. Many different organizations, including schools, districts, universities, and nonprofit organizations, are beginning to issue microcredentials; and some states are even attributing continuing education unit (CEU) credits to the microcredentials. Participants typically have options for the type of artifact (video, lesson plan, picture, reflection) they might submit, but the key is that they have to demonstrate what they have learned. Experts and/or peers review submissions based on a validated rubric.

We mention this idea because if you want to encourage a teacher to pursue a particular area of professional learning or you want your entire team to focus on one area as a school, microcredentials could provide a way for them to learn and make progress at their own pace. One potential for microcredentials is that they can push people to try something they have learned and can also provide a specific reason for teachers to go to the next step with what they have learned.

People do not always earn a microcredential simply because they complete the requirements. This credentialing approach moves away from one of measured seat time to one of demonstrated mastery. Digital badges and microcredentials represent competency-based opportunities for educators to learn and improve their pedagogy. The Friday Institute at North Carolina State, which offers microcredentials in several areas, including learning differences, digital learning, and teaching various math concepts, finds that many people do not earn the credential the first time through the material, but with the feedback they receive, nearly half are successful on the second try. This approach to garnering microcredentials allows teachers to experience the power and potential of competency-based learning.

Derek has used digital badges as a way to provide flexible options for teachers who want to grow, especially around digital learning. In his school's Learning Management System, he provides access to digital badges on some very practical tools and resources to encourage and provide support for teachers who want to learn more. Some teams may tackle some microcredentials together. Digital badges or microcredentials also are available outside of schools and districts. For example, Digital Promise provides a catalog of microcredentials that educators can choose to learn on topics ranging from coaching, learning differences, and the SAMR [Substitution, Augmentation, Modification, Redefinition] framework for integrating technology to classroom management.[7]

CHALLENGE YOUR OWN LEARNING

You can also help your teachers and students see you as a learner—the lead learner. Part of building an effective culture is placing an emphasis on ongoing, job-embedded professional learning. As a leader, you can model the importance of professional learning by taking the time for your own growth and making it a priority. Your teachers may know you are out of the building for a meeting, but if you are out of the building and learning something new, find a way to show or tell them what you learned. For example, if you are at a professional learning session and see a video of what personalized learning can look like, consider showing that video to your team at a faculty or a PLC meeting and pose some guiding questions. You can also use Twitter to share what you're learning in real time. Put your own learning out there and make it visible for everyone to see.

You also have the chance to show that informal professional learning matters—and is important—by modeling your own use. If you learn something on Twitter, share the resource and reference that your own PLN provided you with this information. If a teacher asks a question that you don't know the answer to, suggest that the teacher or you put that question out on Twitter or another platform to see what others might offer as an answer and then bring the responses back and share them. Some educators emphasize that their teachers should build a PLN in and beyond the school. It's important to remember that informal professional learning can take on many different shapes and sizes.

TRY IT TOMORROW

1. **Effective professional learning must be ongoing, job-embedded, and relevant.** It must help connect with peers, but it can also look very different and be formal or informal. As the principal, you have the opportunity not only to model your own learning but also to recognize, encourage, and point to a wide range of opportunities. You will not reach your vision without effective professional learning, and investing in professional learning that encourages trying new things and trust will only help you build your effective culture and reach your goals. One idea for modeling life-long learning is to encourage your staff to participate in a Twitter chat. Seeing you participating in the chat and gaining new resources and ideas from others who are participating will help you build a culture of learners. Cyberman has a good list of chats as well as tips for participating in a chat.[8]

2. **Make time at faculty meetings or during regular staff gatherings to have teachers share something new that they have learned or a great resource they have found through professional reading or social media.** Making this time to honor and share new learning builds a culture of life-long learning and collaboration. It also encourages teachers to learn outside traditional professional development.

6

Empower Students
with the Four Cs

*My vision is that teachers leverage their resources—
textbooks, written materials, outside folks—to be able to
provide an education for students where students build their
own capacity to be agents for themselves. For me, it's really
important that we have an education that not just ensures
that kids are career and college ready, but that also makes
them productive citizens so that they can make good choices
when they're voting and when they're out in the community.*

—ERIN FREW

ook deeply at your personal vision for teaching and learning, and it is
likely that themes related to empowering students, developing ownership
of learning, and engaging the Four Cs (collaboration, critical thinking, communication, and creativity) emerge. For many educators, the idea of empowering students or developing learner agency provides a lens that makes sense
for teachers and students. We know now more than ever that students need
to be able to understand how to learn and how to approach new situations.
Simply regurgitating information will not ensure their success in college,
career, or citizenship. Many different instructional strategies and even school
culture norms can be utilized to place an emphasis on the student-centered
approach to learning. These strategies may include project-based learning,

Genius Hour, student tech teams, or self-directed learning opportunities and may also encompass areas such as learning environments, assessments, and connections to the community.

Several key areas emerge as we consider how to empower learners. Here we examine each of these areas and provide examples of schools and educators who are excelling in these areas. If one or many of these examples resonate with you, you will be able to connect your teachers with resources and research to help support your efforts:

- Help students understand their own learning.
- Develop opportunities for learner agency.
- Embed the Four Cs throughout teaching and learning.
- Recognize student ownership and the Four Cs through assessments and sharing.
- Create collaborative learning spaces.

HELP STUDENTS UNDERSTAND THEIR OWN LEARNING

Often students go through the day-to-day motions of schools without stopping and thinking about the idea of learning, and it is rare that they are given the opportunity to reflect on their own learning. Students are task oriented, concerned with whatever assignment is due next and how much time they have to complete it. They typically measure progress through grades, not content learned. One of the most effective strategies to support students in understanding their learning is metacognition, or the skill of thinking about your own thinking and learning. John Hattie identifies teaching metacognitive skills as one of the high-impact-evident, evidence-based strategies in his meta-analysis of over a half-million research studies on student outcomes.[1] Building in time and strategies for student reflection is a critical step in the learning process. We should also guide students in discovering their own learning strengths and differences. Giving them a language to use and discover how they learn most effectively is exciting and empowering (and sometimes even fun).

Allowing students to begin to identify how they learn also encourages them to understand that all students learn differently. Hattie identifies teaching metacognitive skills as one of the most high-impact, evidence-based strategies. Unfortunately, many students think that learning in prescribed ways is better than learning in other ways. This idea is often tied to the more traditional view of schooling because students who learn in certain ways—memorizing or by showing what they know on a multiple-choice test—are rewarded in most schools. One strategy to help students see and understand that all types of learning are valuable and effective is to help them have language to talk about their learning. Many years ago, the way to do so may have been through quizzes around preferences or strengths for learning in a visual, auditory, and kinesthetic way. We used quick quizzes and encouraged students to talk about how they learned, and we discussed strategies that students might use when studying or talking to a teacher. These relatively simple approaches helped students talk about what they needed but did not get at the heart of students' learning differences or strengths because learning is more complex and nuanced; many additional factors affect learning, in addition to the learning styles of visual, kinesthetic, and auditory.

Another simple strategy that we have employed with groups of adults or students is to use a digital tool like Socrative or Kahoot (Socrative provides more answer options) to do a large group quiz that is anonymous to the group. We ask a set of questions one by one to show the diverse answers to each question throughout the room. This approach could be used early in a school year to demonstrate that all learners, including teachers, learn differently. Asking these questions gets the conversation about learning preferences and learning differences started. Questions like the ones we developed and have included in the sample "Learning Preferences Quiz" also provide important insight for teachers into how students learn. This insight can provide a glimpse or even a data point for how to understand ways to personalize for each student.

Committing the time to and having these types of discussions early, and repeating them periodically, can reap dividends in the long run as students begin to think about and understand, based on the teacher's modeling, what reflection about learning means. You can model this behavior by having your teachers complete a quiz like this at the beginning of the school year or before school starts. Your teachers will enjoy seeing how they are alike and different from the others in your school. We also find that only one or two adults in the room think that a multiple-choice test best shows their learning, which is an important discussion point for teachers as they consider alternative or formative assessments. You can then share the exact quiz with your teachers

LEARNING PREFERENCES QUIZ: EXAMPLE

1. If given the opportunity to participate in one of the following learning situations, which would you choose?
   a. large group instruction
   b. small group instruction/collaboration
   c. virtual instruction
   d. gaming
   e. independent practice
   f. one-on-one instruction with a teacher

2. When I get frustrated, I need to take a break from what I'm doing.
   a. yes
   b. no

3. If given a time of day or night to learn, which would you choose?
   a. 5:00 a.m.–9:00 a.m.
   b. 9:00 a.m.–1:00 p.m.
   c. 1:00 p.m.–6:00 p.m.
   d. 6:00 p.m.–11:00 p.m.
   e. 11:00 p.m.–5:00 a.m.

4. I need to finish one task before starting another.
   a. yes
   b. no

5. What type of assessment would best reflect what you have learned? (Or how do you best like to show what you have learned?)
   a. multiple-choice test
   b. project with multiple components
   c. open-ended essay
   d. task-oriented, performance-based assessment
   e. oral, artistic, or visual presentation

6. Where do you like to learn best?
   a. in a quiet classroom with desks
   b. walking or moving around
   c. in a coffee shop with lots of noise around me
   d. on my couch at home with my dog or cat sitting next to me
   e. sitting outside
   f. in a bustling classroom with tables and comfortable chairs

and staff, making it available for them to revise or refine and use with their students. This process lets teachers know that you value this work and that you want them to engage in metacognition with their students.

While the field is evolving almost every day, neurocognitive science provides us with more in-depth and science-backed ways to discuss learning. The tools to use with students more generally, however, are still somewhat limited. One early tool that we have used with students, especially those in middle and high school, is called the Learner Sketch by the QED Foundation.[2] While this easy-to-use and engaging tool is not perfect, it provides students with a peek at some of their learning preferences by asking them to identify whether a description "is really me" or "is not me." The students immediately get a "report" of their learning. This tool is also effective for adults. Schools can set up a school account so that they can share aggregated data to make the case that many different types of learners are found across the class or the school.

Whatever tools you employ to help students think about their learning will provide a language that you can continue to use. If students express frustration about how they studied but did not perform well on a test, you may be able talk about their Learner Sketch results or their learning preferences or differences as a way to help them improve. Talking about learning and having students and teachers see that each student learns differently also change the culture in the classroom—and building—and make it more acceptable for students to have and acknowledge different strengths and challenges. When these differences are out in the open and everyone is able to talk about them, students begin to feel more successful and accepted.

Research demonstrates the importance of helping students understand and reflect on their own learning. Fadel, Trilling, and Bialik explain that metacognition is transferrable in that it improves the application of what is learned beyond the immediate task:

> Metacognition can be developed in students in the context of their current goals and can enhance their learning of competencies as well as transfer of learning, no matter their starting achievement level. In fact, it may be most useful for lower-achieving students, as the higher-achieving students are already employing strategies that have proven successful for them. For learning disabled and low-achieving students, metacognitive training has been shown to improve behavior more effectively than traditional attention-control training.

Students who have higher levels of self-efficacy (more confidence in their ability to achieve their goals) are more likely to engage in metacognition and, in turn, are more likely to perform at higher levels. This strongly indicates a positive feedback loop for high-achieving students—they are more successful by using metacognitive strategies, which increases their confidence and in turn leads them to continue to increase their performance. Metacognition is an integral part of this virtuous learning cycle, and one that is amenable to further improvement through instruction.[3]

Interestingly, we often don't take time to develop these skills in the students who are struggling the most because we are afraid to take time away from the content itself. We sell our students short when we don't believe that they can learn how to think about their own learning, and we further the gap when we don't help the students learn how to reflect as a strategy to improve their learning.

One strategy for encouraging metacognition that can work for students of all ages, even in kindergarten, is student-led conferences. This approach completely changes the traditional conference to which the student is not even invited and certainly plays no part in sharing learning and goals. Former principal Michael Armstrong's school utilized student-led conferences along with student portfolios and/or data notebooks so that the students were using data to share their learning story and to provide a rationale for their goals:

> One of my favorite takeaways from Bugg [Creative Arts Magnet School] was flipped instruction with student-led conferences. During this process students created a video each quarter where they shared their goals and their accomplishments. I have videos of my own son where he is talking about his goals. It's a great use of using a digital tool to capture that information. Having students talk about their learning and share with their parents and other adults about where they are with their goals and how they plan to accomplish the goals they have yet to reach really empowers kids. And seeing the growth from the beginning of the year to the end of the year in the videos is amazing!

Another approach used by teachers in principal Amy Rickard's school is having students talk about their own learning and their own assessments. The third-grade team specifically had students complete a reflection about their math assessment. Often students take a test and may not see or hear about it for weeks. Sometimes it disappears forever. They may get back the test or a just a test score, but they are typically not guided or taught how to go back and look over the test and understand their own learning or challenges. Students at Morris Grove Elementary School are asked to write about what they did not understand and think about how they can make sure to continue on to master the content. The students then talk about what they wrote and their reflections with their teacher. These are eight-year-old students learning how to reflect and then create a plan for improvement. Amy says,

> We have seen more from the district on math—with metacognition and re-flection—helping kids talk about their thinking. I wish I had learned math the way they teach it now. Getting kids to explain their thinking solidifies learning. This is helping kids with the metacognition piece and building foundation.

This approach also creates a safe space in which students can share their challenges, and their teachers have the chance to model reflection and goal setting without being punitive. Metacognition does not simply happen. Students (and adults) need guidance and practice on how to effectively think about their learning.

Former principal Troy Moore's personalized pathways across grade levels pushed students to understand their own learning. Students in his school talked about what they were learning, where they were on their pathways, the choices they made on those pathways, and where they were going. These students had a deep understanding of their goals and why they wanted to work hard to get to the next standard or pathway. About this type of approach, Troy says,

> I believe a well-developed Personalized Pathway per objective or common objective that provides each student with a healthy balance of digital instruction, one-on-one conferencing opportunities with the instructional staff, student choice, and the availability of progressing at his/her own pace fosters student agency. Some students get extremely motivated by seeing the layout of the grade level pathways for the year (in hopes to move to the next grade level's pathways), while others heighten their engagement due to choice in interest-based PBLs and scenario-based performance tasks.

Sometimes we assume high school students understand their learning or know how to address challenges, but former principal Erin Frew and her teachers made a purposeful choice to help students be able to talk about their learning as a way to show what they learned and understand what it takes for them to be prepared. Erin says,

> One of the things we've worked hard on over the past one and a half years is *having students know their own learning story.* We've involved the kids in thinking about "Where I was when I came in, and what is my goal for the year? How am I going to grow? What are the things I'm going to do?" The tenth-grade geometry teacher has them do a learning log. "What have I learned this week? What have I done to contribute to my own learning? What could I have done differently? What can I do differently next week?" This has led to huge increases in the winter NWEA assessment. The students know who they are and what they do. She also uses Khan Academy and CK–12 to personalize and meet them where they are. She leverages resources, and they have their own roadmap. They get credit not just for completion, but for the time they put in. If they do the one hundred active minutes, they get credit. The teacher rewards effort, because some have a slower pace, emphasizing growth.

DEVELOP OPPORTUNITIES FOR LEARNER AGENCY

As you look at instruction that is moving toward personalized and student-centered learning, you will likely see commonalities around learner agency. Learner agency means that students have ownership of and the ability to drive their own learning. This type of learning is often described as "voice and choice," but it goes beyond that and includes the experience itself. On their website, Barbara Bray and Kathleen McClaskey share several continua to help explain what this looks like in practice, including the continua of voice, choice, and engagement.[4] Principals who are implementing effective personalized and digital learning are building student agency and empowering students as learners through their everyday actions and the culture they build in their schools.

John Bernia, former principal at Carleton Middle School, changed the tone and approach to learning through the questions he asked. "I always start, whether with student or student and parents, by asking them, 'Tell me where you are trying to go.' I listen, and we go from there. By the end, I have probably met with every student and had a conversation. I have one child who checks in every day."

The example of student-led conferences to support metacognition can also significantly help build learner agency. Students who have never before led or even had a conversation about their own learning goals are suddenly in the driver's seat. This approach almost always helps parents or guardians see their children in a different way, and it also opens doors for future discussions about how students are progressing on their goals or how to support learning differences. Adding this component will take work for teachers, especially in the beginning, but as students learn about how to lead conferences and practice, they will become more and more capable of leading them. Consistency across the grades in a school or even across the schools in a district allows students to build this capacity that will help them in college, career, and citizenship—both in being able to share and advocate for themselves but also in understanding the paths and options.

Superintendent Suzanne Lacey and her district and school leaders have built learner agency and leadership into every aspect of their work, including for elementary, middle, and high school students:

> We need to give kids a stage—and part of this is about expectations. As adults, we set expectations. We set expectations for what kids do and how they do it, and this has revitalized our school system for the kids. In our elementary schools, we have done work with the Leader in Me (Covey). It's perfectly aligned with what we wanted to do with teaching and learning. That built so much ownership and leadership in kids. They build their leadership notebook. It builds their capacity to own their learning.
>
> We have student-led conferences. Their props are the leadership notebook, with their learning, discipline, and successes. For students to be able to conduct conferences is amazing, and parents are so appreciative. Who else should own their learning but the kids? This has built confidence and increased leadership. We have this in all of our elementary schools. We now have four of the schools that are lighthouse status—and next year, two more. I am proud because it has been an investment, but a perfect complement for what we are trying to do.
>
> What we have done in all of our schools, K–12, is the student leadership teams. That continues to serve dual roles as far as leadership. Students act as ambassadors and hosts/hostesses. They help advise on decisions that affect their schools. They work with principals. They articulate their learning and talk about their schools the way adults talk about it. This is a natural connection by virtue of the expectations in the classroom.

Amy emphasizes learner agency in professional learning and discussions with her teachers as a way to consider equity:

The growth mindset and PBIS [Positive Behavioral Intervention and Supports] support our focus as a school to build upon the positive and strengths as a culture. One of the most powerful things we've done is read the book *Choice Words* (Peter Johnson). We read it one of the first years as a school. There is a whole chapter on student agency, and we took it from an equity lens. How do you name what children are doing to create agency? This has translated to having strong dialogues with kids. Relationships are huge. We try to emphasize, and are most proud of, when people say, "This school is so positive. Everyone is so happy." Kids feel that.

Tim Lauer, former principal of Meriwether Lewis Elementary School, applied a similar strategy to ensure that his teachers were empowered to provide choice and flexibility to improve a student's agency:

In terms of agency, I try to help teachers understand that students come with a lot of knowledge and have skill sets that exceed their teachers with technology—utilizing them as teachers in the classroom, teachers of each other, and supporting staff. Also, highlighting students' work is really important and making sure they have opportunities to share. One student was making a video project and had teachers utilize him as the expert. The teacher pointed students to him to help the others.

Tim also emphasizes that the design of the learning environment can be an important way to support learner agency, especially for students who may have trouble focusing in a traditional "desks in a row" model. This learning environment, Tim says, applies to the instruction, as well as the physical space:

Some teachers have been very open and brought in resources of their own, creating standing or sitting areas, using tables that adjust. Or letting students who need more quiet to go in the hallway. We are boxes and hallways, but we've tried to provide more seating and spaces in the school to encourage students to flow out of the room and make the space your own. But, when you take people into the space, it can feel hodgepodge, and when the students are busy, it looks disjointed. It needs to be a space that has a flow.

Similar to Tim, Troy focused on learning spaces. While he applied this focus in an elementary school, the ideas around learning spaces are absolutely applicable to middle and high school. Consider how students like coffee shops or comfortable chairs. If you can create these environments in your school, you can make it more appealing to students and also encourage collaboration. Troy says,

I also believe the physical environment within the classroom encourages student agency. At Hawk Ridge, we launched a campaign to remove the traditional desks from our building. In six weeks, we had sent over seven hundred desks back to the district warehouse and outfitted most of our rooms with lightweight tables that could be moved easily, and with stools and soft seating. The teachers were encouraged to solicit student voice in the design. Some rooms developed themes such as a family room setting, a dining room setting, outdoor patio setting, twenty-first century modern, etc. We were able to fund this by working with our PTA, to take in classroom donations for individual classrooms, and to allow the teachers to buy based on the donations received for their room. Students and teachers sent out master plans for their rooms to develop a buzz to solicit the donations. Some classrooms partnered up to use the tutor room in between them to make a functioning library run by the students. Ideas like these give teachers the flexibility to be very creative and to communicate to the students that this environment is yours. Own it and do great things for yourself and others!

Troy also added Genius Hour as a norm for all students in his school. Genius Hour is a designated time in which students have the opportunity to work together or work alone and change their preferences based on the project. This approach includes a focus on each student's passions with a focus on exploring and creating. It is also related to the concept of 20% Time, which originated at Google, where employees were encouraged to spend 20 percent of their time on pet projects. These approaches encourage innovation, engagement, and entrepreneurial opportunities.

At Hawk Ridge, students had dedicated time at the beginning of the school day two or three times per week. Students in Troy's schools shared projects ranging from a gymnastics club for younger students to Claymation videos to a series of podcasts with music. Digital learning played a role in many, but not all, of the projects; and some of the projects took a week, whereas others like the podcast series ran over the entire year. Students talked about their passions and how they had started by brainstorming what they cared about and then talked with teachers because it was helpful and worked with other students to develop their ideas. One student shared that he had a passion for music, and another girl in his class had a passion for technology, so they put their passions together to develop a radio podcast series. Teachers played an important role in facilitating these students' learning. Because projects began and ended on a rolling schedule, teachers were able to have one-on-one or small group time with many students, allowing them to personalize the learning. For some teachers, Genius Hour helped them understand what was possible with personalized pathways and the capacity of students to have ownership of their learning.

Metacognition and agency have similarities across all grade levels, but they may also take on different forms. Principal Alison Hramiec, from Boston Day and Evening Academy, shares how her students are able to own their learning, their pathways, and their goals by guiding and expecting students to understand and talk about their learning through their competency-based approach to learning. The Four Cs are also prevalent in the day-to-day work. While some of these aspects may make more sense for high school, other strategies of a competency-based approach could also support elementary and middle school students, according to Alison:

> [Competency based learning] may present in one's mind a vision of students working independently and at their own pace. At BDEA, we know that college and career readiness requires more than content knowledge. Students must also learn how to be collaborative with their peers, be creative problem solvers, think critically, and communicate effectively and professionally. When visitors visit our classrooms, they see very similar practices to what they would see in our traditional engaging classrooms. Students read and analyze text as a class; they stand in front of their peers to present solutions to math problems; they work collaboratively on experiments, sharing data and drawing conclusions. Personalized learning does not mean individualized learning. Personalization at BDEA is making sure students are in classes learning new and relevant skills and content.

EMBED THE FOUR CS THROUGHOUT TEACHING AND LEARNING

Collaboration, critical thinking, communication, and creativity are the skills students need to be successful in the twenty-first century. These are not new skills. Teachers have long been using and developing these skills in classrooms. What's different now is the emphasis and the amount of in-school time spent developing these skills. Communication tools and strategies have changed enormously over the past two or three decades. Today people are constantly connected and constantly communicating, using tools such as Twitter, Snapchat, and Instagram. These communication vehicles have changed the nature of communication, and we are now trained to think in short bursts, sometimes with only words but just as often with pictures and captions. A high degree of creativity is involved in these communications because the audience can be quite large, and we have many tools to choose from when composing a note. There is pressure to be thoughtful, witty, and creative.

The nature of collaboration has changed also. It is no longer limited to the assigned group project, culminating in a group presentation. Collaboration can be a constant, both in the classroom and beyond. Students can collaborate while finding answers, writing paragraphs, and doing labs. But these collaborations are not limited to their classroom peers. They can collaborate with educators and students from around the globe in real time. And because the world has opened up through these enhanced capabilities to communicate and collaborate, the emphasis on critical thinking has also become more prominent. Because so much information is available and so many connections have to be made, it's important to have strong critical thinking skills to manage the integration of it all.

The Four Cs provide a tangible and important framework for ensuring that students are empowered to reach their potential in this changing world and for preparing students for college, career, and citizenship. It is difficult to disagree with the importance of the Four Cs, but depending on pressures around high-stakes testing or pacing guides, the Four Cs can be an aspect of instruction that teachers leave out or skip over when they run out of time. The ideas of collaboration, communication, critical thinking, and creativity often resonate with educators because they make sense. However, if educators don't implement them carefully and with intention, students may have only a superficial exposure to these competencies. When instruction is more teacher-directed, the Four Cs are often glossed over or addressed only sporadically rather than as an integral part of teaching and learning.

When the Four Cs are addressed purposefully, students can develop a strong skill set and also have more in-depth learning opportunities with the standards themselves. In many states, the standards now specifically address the Four Cs. Many other districts have utilized the Four Cs as a way to improve instruction. If your state is one of these, consider addressing and emphasizing their use with your teachers. Amy brings the idea of the Four Cs back to the standards because teachers need to have a deep understanding of the standards to be prepared to develop lessons that encourage metacognition and agency, while also addressing the Four Cs. Whether a variation of Common Core State Standards (CCSS) or the state's own standards, college- and career-ready standards lend—and some would argue, require—the integration of the Four Cs. The work needed to unpack the standards effectively—with content and pedagogical knowledge, while also understanding the role that digital learning and the Four Cs play—is not easy, but the opportunity to improve student outcomes is worth the effort. Amy says,

> It's an exciting time. The standards are well written. Now, teachers know what they are supposed to teach and what children are supposed to learn. We are designing work that is at a high level. We see well-designed work for kids—quality work. The speaking and listening standards, and work on accountable talk, have given kids [a] real voice and a shift in students being active in their learning. When teachers are designing better work for kids, then you see opportunities for choice. They are finding ways to make standards exciting for kids.

Principal Derek McCoy focuses his efforts around learning environments in his middle school on designing collaborative spaces, emphasizing the importance of the Four Cs every day. In West Rowan, the hallways are called collaborative spaces. They are painted and decorated. Derek tries to model this flexibility in learning space and emphasis on the Four Cs but appreciates that his superintendent and district leadership also encourage the adults in the system to engage in and implement the Four Cs. He says, "[Superintendent] Dr. Moody comes in or has her executive director visit the schools, and they ask instructional questions. They make sure that the framework and blueprint are in place —and that's it. They tell us to get creative. They make it work. It's liberating." This is a great example of how you can model for your teachers. If you encourage them to be creative, to collaborate, and to think creatively, you are modeling what you want them to do for students every day.

EMPHASIZE THE IMPORTANCE OF THE FOUR CS

You have an opportunity to emphasize the importance of the Four Cs with your teachers by using the Four Cs as a lens for your more informal walk-throughs. You could design a quick Google form to provide immediate feedback to teachers a couple of times a week or at any regular interval. The form might include a check box for each of the Four Cs, and you can indicate which ones you saw in action during your short visit. You could also have a text box to share some quick comments with positive reinforcement, with a suggestion, or with a note about wanting to talk more because you liked what you saw but see some other opportunities. The Google form provides you with a way to e-mail the teacher right away. If you prefer handwritten feedback, you can print a form to share similar information. A benefit of the Google form is that you can set it up in a way to track the feedback for all your teachers over time and see how they are growing in their application of the Four Cs.

RECOGNIZE STUDENT OWNERSHIP AND THE FOUR CS THROUGH ASSESSMENTS AND SHARING

Making learner agency, metacognition, and the Four Cs an integral part of your vision for teaching and learning can help personalize learning and empower students on a daily basis and in an ongoing way. For many students, developing learner agency in school and focusing on the skills embedded in the Four Cs lead to changes in how they see themselves as students and the goals they set for themselves.

One former superintendent in Floydada, Texas, Jerry Vaughn, utilized personalized and digital learning over a decade ago to connect his students, many of them first-generation Americans, to experiences beyond what was available in his district. This effort included connections with NASA and engineering programs that led the students to interacting with experts and peers from across the country. The experiences and the changes to instruction and use of digital learning collectively allowed the students to develop the Four Cs and then apply them. Vaughn also made sure that students in his high school (which was seventy miles from the closest community college) had access to college courses. He explained, "If they don't start, they won't ever graduate." He helped students see themselves as capable, as able to compete nationally, and as college students. Once they knew they could compete, they wanted to continue. Vaughn's district not only incorporated learner agency and the Four Cs into the instruction but also emphasized sharing what the students were learning and their successes.

Highlighting students' agency and the products they develop by applying the Four Cs is one way to emphasize the importance of them to all students, teachers, parents, and the community. Having stakeholders participate in the sharing of what students produce as expert reviewers or as an audience for a presentation or having them visit schools to see students' ownership of their own learning in action can become your most powerful advocacy tool. Michael reminds us that events can play an important role for the parents and community, but also for students: "The other thing is that doing an event is big and empowering for the kids. Even if the teachers don't want to do the events, kids like events. Kids get excited about that. Those events allow kids to show off and that's a reason to have them."

Events are a lot of work, especially for teachers and administrators, but they can also be core to the instruction. They can include a music show or holiday singing, but they can also be more content driven and interactive. When students collaborate to create and then have to figure out how to share, they often practice all of the Four Cs. They have to be creative to decide what they want to do; they almost always collaborate to create, build, or plan. Ideally, they also are using critical thinking to solve the challenge of having only a limited amount of time or needing to involve many adults, and they absolutely have to communicate with an authentic audience. Events can also open the dialogue for people in the community, but especially parents. Parents can often go much deeper in conversation when they have a shared experience to build on, and they also know more about what to ask their children at home because they understand their capacity for discussion about learning.

These are the stories that you want to share: students, from preK to seniors, are incredibly capable of learning and talking about their own learning. Once stakeholders hear students expound on what they have learned and how they were actively involved in creating knowledge and products, the stakeholders begin to understand the difference between teacher-directed and more person-alized, student-centered learning. Digital learning can provide many different avenues to sharing work and also to the products that students can create.

Alternative assessments can also support the Four Cs and learner agency. As you move toward personalized and digital learning, moving away from multiple-choice assessments can help make the learning more student-centered. Providing more than one way for students to demonstrate their learning creates more ownership in the learning, requires students to be able to reflect on their own learning, and also allows teachers to gain a better understanding of what students really know and are able to do better than one prescribed, narrow approach allows.

CREATE COLLABORATIVE LEARNING SPACES

Our environment matters. A warm and welcome space that is bright and colorful can draw us in just as easily as a dark and dreary space can evoke negative emotions. Learning spaces can shape teaching and learning and also can support a positive school culture. As we examine ways that educators can engage students, we would be remiss if we didn't also look at learning spaces as a critical component to engaging and empowering students.

During a school visit a few years ago, we traveled to an economically depressed area in our state, where nearly all the schools in the district were considered to be "failing." We had visited many other schools in this district, but as we stepped foot onto this campus, we could tell something was different. The feeling we got when we walked into the office was energizing. As we walked into the main lobby, we saw a mural of a scene from *Harry Potter*. Later, when we walked into the cafeteria, we saw mural scenes with life-size characters from *Alice in Wonderland* and *The Wizard of Oz*. The classrooms were decorated in themes of camping, Disney, and space, all depicted through murals and accompanying decorations. Students in the classrooms worked in small groups, while others rehearsed rap songs they had written prior to taking a math quiz.

The principal of this school wanted teachers to personalize their classrooms with murals because he knew paint was inexpensive and the paintings would give a much-needed face-lift to the aging school. But more importantly, he felt strongly that allowing teachers to personalize their rooms would really get them to buy in to the idea that the learning environment is important. After enlisting the help of the art teacher and a few former students, each teacher selected a theme and then during the summer, the art teacher painted a mural in their room to help represent that theme. Teachers then carried out the theme on their bulletin boards and in other fun ways so that when the next school year started, the school was a transformed space. Although several changes were taking place at this school, the teachers were filled with a unique buy-in to the vision, and it was obvious that what had started as some paint and a theme had spilled over into classroom instruction.

Building a culture of innovation and personalization takes time, but starting with the physical space can set the tone. We have provided many examples of how efforts to build learner agency can have direct demands on or respond to the learning environment itself. For example, collaborative spaces that look like coffee shops or have comfortable seating can encourage students to work together in an ongoing and organic way. Providing interactive and creation spaces in the media center changes the library from a quiet, individual environment to one in which learning may involve collaborating and creating. Classrooms that move away from desks in a row almost immediately signal a shift away from a teacher-directed approach. Obviously, the instruction and learning must respond to these changes, but the environment can help teachers and students begin to envision learning in new ways.

As you build a culture to support this personalized and digital learning, consider how the learning environment can help students and teachers have pride in their school and also help them see that they are trusted to interact and work together. Think about how updating the teachers' lounge and other spaces for educators—whether through paint, some new color, or some other means that facilitate learning—may also strengthen their view of themselves as professionals in this culture that encourages the growth mindset and a willingness to take risks. Ask students and teachers to give input into what the environment needs and give them opportunities to lead the redesign efforts. Your focus on this aspect of the learning environment is one more way in which you can model and empower students as well as teachers in your transition to personalized and digital learning.

TRY IT TOMORROW

1. **Learning Preferences Quiz.** During a faculty meeting or at the beginning of your next professional development day, create a learning preferences quiz using Kahoot or Socrative and the questions located in the first part of this chapter. After your staff engages with the quiz, use these guiding questions to debrief the quiz:
   - What do you think about the diversity of your responses?
   - If we were to ask students to respond to this quiz, predict what their responses might look like.
   - How do students' different learning styles impact your lesson planning?

2. **Modeling the Four Cs.** We all know the power of modeling. During a professional development day or a faculty meeting, model for your teachers the power the Four Cs

have in engaging learners. With the help of your administrative team or some teacher leaders, set up stations addressing the topics you were planning to cover during the staff meeting. Make sure the stations allow your teachers the time and the opportunity to interact with the content and utilize the Four Cs. After you're finished with the rotations, debrief the experience with your staff. Ask them if they liked learning in that way versus how they have traditionally engaged in staff meetings. Challenge your staff to create an activity that engages students in new ways, in particular utilizing the Four Cs, during the next two weeks. Don't forget to follow up with staff members at a later faculty meeting, asking them to share their classroom experiences.

3. **Learning Spaces.** Share a video from Edutopia featuring Albemarle Public Schools.[5] After watching the video, ask teachers to discuss how the learning spaces they saw in the video helped foster the Four Cs and learner agency. Have the teachers brainstorm how they can use the furniture they already have to create learning spaces that engage students and promote the Four Cs.

7

Create Systems and Structures That Are Sustainable and Adaptable

I'm always thinking, "If I left tomorrow, what would happen?" I never want to be the guy who leaves and everything falls apart. I'm always striving to create an environment where our teachers have enough ownership and know what to do so they would be fine without me. The more voices in the field and the more people I incorporate, the better chance it is that they have ownership.

—JOHN BERNIA

We have not focused heavily on devices or technology thus far in the book. This may seem strange since the focus of the book is the transition to personalized and digital learning. We have certainly explained when technological devices have supported the vision of personalized learning, but our reason for waiting until this point in the book was to ensure that we did not fall into the trap of leading the transition discussion with devices or technology. Instead, we have focused on teaching and learning. Devices and technology do matter, but they will not fix poor teaching or instructional strategies. Solidify your vision for learning and instruction first.

Many districts or schools enter this transition to personalized and digital learning with access to one-time funding for technology. This funding often comes without a systemic plan built on a vision and without supports. Building in a plan for and systems that support the sustainability of your vision is critical for long-term success and improvements in student outcomes. In your work with stakeholders, teachers, and students, you should consider the technology and systems themselves, as well as how those systems will impact the sustainability of your vision. Build a plan that allows for the evolution of your vision and the ever-changing resources, technologies, and systems that are available. *Do not* build a plan around devices! Technology and digital tools are constantly changing. The current or cutting edge today will likely be outdated in two to three years. Don't wait for the next best thing because you might never make decisions or move forward. *Do* make your plan and vision allow for the evolution of systems and devices to better meet your needs as time progresses. Balancing the present needs with the idea of changing needs can be tough, but it's important to remember that change is the new normal. Technologies will change. Systems will change. Your vision for what your school and community need will change. Your financial investments in systems and technology are not permanent. You will need to upgrade and add and possibly even change course entirely at some point. You need to work with your district or other funding sources to create a plan for ongoing funding and line items that support these efforts. Buying the devices is not the end of costs. You will have maintenance and updates, and some devices will break and need to be replaced. The key is that you plan with your technology leaders—in your building, at the district level, or possibly with your corporate partners—to be prepared so that you can continue supporting and sustaining your vision for learning and not disrupt progress with teachers and students.

Discussions and actions around the technology, infrastructure, and systems themselves often raise fears among stakeholders due to child safety and appropriateness. Parents may be concerned about the amount of screen time their children will have at school and their ability to access dangerous content. Teachers may be worried about students staying focused on the instruction and not simply browsing the Internet. These are valid concerns, and you have the opportunity to help students and their families learn and practice how to be safe and responsible online through a comprehensive digital citizenship program. For example, many districts have documented positive outcomes that you can share.[1]

Teachers must embed digital citizenship into their lessons and activities and explicitly teach students about Internet safety and what it means to be a good digital citizen. Just like we teach children how to safely cross a street or how to be good citizens in our classroom, teachers must show students how to be good citizens outside the classroom and how to use reliable resources to find information. As the lead learner in your building, you can help your teachers come up with a plan of action for ensuring that these skills are being taught. Promoting good digital citizenship is one more avenue to empowering students, and addressing this issue head-on and involving parents, students, teachers, and the community members from the beginning will make a big difference in helping stakeholders see that learning how to access and use digital information in context at school can help students throughout their daily activities and lives.

One of your roles as the principal is to ensure that teachers, students, and other educators have what they need to achieve your shared vision for teaching and learning. You may have some opportunity and flexibility to make decisions around content and devices, so you should model that those decisions are always made with the vision for teaching and learning at the forefront. Even if you do not have autonomy for purchases, you can have an impact on the choices by understanding what is working in your school and what is not effective so that you can share that information back with the district. The following are key areas for you to consider:

- access (in school and at home)
- digital content and resources
- devices
- funding for sustainability and partnering with your district
- digital citizenship

You may feel you have little control in these areas, but developing a more in-depth understanding of each of them will allow you to advocate for what you need to meet your vision for teaching and learning. This will also help you better understand what may be frustrating or getting in the way of your teachers and students from maximizing the potential of teaching and learning.

ACCESS (IN SCHOOL AND AT HOME)

We have all become dependent on Internet access and expect to have it nearly everywhere we go. We have a hard time retrieving calendars, saving documents, getting directions, or communicating with each other without wireless access. Despite this reality, we often ask teachers to thoughtfully integrate technology and digital content without adequate and reliable access. If a teacher has planned a lesson that depends on technology and the technology or the access fails, she is likely to try *only one more time* before deciding that using technology is not worth the effort, unless she is working with a coach or she's seen how an administrator or coach handled a similar situation. The way a teacher approaches the challenges of utilizing technology varies greatly depending on the culture of the school, the growth mindset (or lack thereof) of the teacher, and the supports the teacher has in place. Good teachers are flexible and can change plans on the fly, but if they are at that vulnerable point of learning how to integrate technology effectively, having things go wrong at least twice may convince them not to try again. This is especially true when they are already worried about not covering the material adequately or feeling the demands of a pacing guide.

Access includes not only the ability to connect to the Internet but also the ability to access learning opportunities. Access should be a primary goal in moving to personalized and digital learning—increasing access in terms of timing (24/7), courses (online or blended), or pacing or type of content. Increased access is often achieved, or at least supported, through digital learning and being connected to the Internet. Many groups have set goals in terms of the connectivity needs for a school. For example, the State Educational Technology Directors Association, with the input of many experts and stakeholders, has set the goal that schools should have the following by 2020–2021 (with lower goals in between now and then):

- *Small School Districts* (fewer than 1,000 students): At least 4.3 Mbps per user
- *Medium School District Size* (3,000 students): At least 3.0 Gbps per 1,000 users
- *Large School District* (more than 10,000 students): At least 2.0 Gbps per 1,000 users[2]

Share these access goals, and the ones for earlier years, with your district or technology leaders or your Internet providers. These national standards have been reviewed by the FCC. You can also share the *Broadband Imperative II* report with these technology and district leaders. These access goals may seem high, even to the technology gurus or your chief technology officer, but they address a reality that in middle and high schools, in particular, most students have their own personal devices (smartphones) that they are connecting to the Internet, even if you provide a device for them. In thinking about access goals, consider the number of devices that will be used as well as the demands placed on Internet use. For example, if students or classes will be streaming videos, the access demand will increase dramatically. Feedback from your teachers will help you understand their usage demands and whether or not they feel they have the connectivity they need.

Teachers must be able to access what they need, when they need it, and with a fast-enough connection. You can get reports from your district CTO or your access provider (if you lead a charter school or are expected to provide and maintain your own access) in terms of the demands as they see them. Ideally, you will also be able to see when demand surpasses what is available so that you can see when and how this is happening. This is another place where focus groups can be particularly helpful. You can ask groups of students about the devices they use at school, what they use their connection for and how much is school-related work, and the types of applications they access. You can ask teachers about what is working, what the frustration points are, and what particular needs they have. This focus group strategy can be useful for all aspects of technology and systems.

If you are in a charter school or a district that expects you to maintain your own connectivity, you may be able to act immediately on the information you collect along with the data from usage and demand. If your district handles the relationship with the Internet provider, you will want to share what you learn from the usage data and the focus groups. You could also conduct a survey to allow people to provide anonymous feedback.

The last critical area that is important to consider is home access. Project Tomorrow and other groups have identified a challenge with access at home that they are calling the *homework gap*. Many students, especially those in schools with a higher percentage of students who qualify for free and reduced lunches, do not have adequate access after they leave the school building. Principals should help increase connectivity at home by working with the district or with the community directly. One middle school principal realized that a local church had more than adequate bandwidth and also had a parish hall with tables. The principal asked the church leaders if the church could be a homework hub in the afterschool and evening hours so that students could go there to have access while doing their homework, and the church leaders agreed. Places like Mooresville, North Carolina, decided to work with the community to establish hotspots, in locations such as McDonald's, where students could access the Internet. Community centers or clubhouses that are accessible without additional transportation can also be used for some of the highest-needs students.

Other districts have put additional strategies in place to help address this homework gap. For schools where students have long commutes on buses, routers were added on the buses, and access became available so that students could be productive on the ride to and from school. Some districts strategically park "hotspot" buses in rural or suburban areas so that more students can have access points near the buses. Others have experimented with sending hotspots with a data plan home with students, but this approach takes some education to ensure that students understand the limitations on the data and do not use it in one day, especially when it is meant to cover a month. Some schools have decided to download, or cache, some of their assignments, content, or resources so that students can work on devices without connectivity.

You may want to ask students, parents, and teachers to complete the national SpeakUp survey and work with Project Tomorrow to get their input.[3] You may instead be able to use results from a state or district survey, or you may need to develop and solicit input on your own. Gathering this information will help you understand if you have access gaps that you need to address. Teachers and other stakeholders often see the lack of home access as a barrier in moving to personalized and digital learning, and your work to develop solutions for students to have access outside school will help everyone see a path forward with homework and assignments that require the Four Cs, especially collaboration, communication, and creativity.

DIGITAL CONTENT AND RESOURCES

Digital content and resources are essentials to consider when moving to personalized and digital learning, and standards are the foundation of the development and curation of these assets. Teachers need to know and deeply understand the standards they are teaching. The standards that the state often gives to them help drive instructional decisions. The district or the school curriculum team then has the opportunity to provide resources and curriculum to support the standards. These resources can come as online tools that support standards, videos, or suggested activities. Armed with knowledge of the standards and the curriculum supports, teachers then have the opportunity to be architects in designing lessons that meet their students' needs.

Having the capacity to design lessons is especially important when the district does not provide a curriculum that supports the transition to personalized and digital learning. Teachers are not typically trained to be curriculum designers. Addressing this knowledge deficit head-on helps empower teachers. Teachers will play a role in this development of curriculum, especially in the first year or two of the transition to personalized and digital learning. This is a big part of the reason that teachers say that the first year of the transition is like being a first-year teacher all over again. The instructional strategies and pedagogy are new, but the development and adaptation of content also pose a big challenge. Add to this the importance of addressing learning differences and ideally Universal Design for Learning (UDL), and it is hard to ignore the complexity of the challenge. At this point, you likely will need to remember that we have yet to meet a teacher who wants to go back after making the transition to personalized and digital learning. Understanding how to lead and support having the most effective content and resources is an important role for school and district leaders.

Digital content and resources include subscriptions or purchased software, teacher-created content (including lesson plans), and open educational resources (OER). Almost all the schools and districts that we work with are struggling in some way with this transition from textbooks and print-based materials to digital content and resources. Many have invested heavily; some have tried to move almost solely to OER and teacher-created content. The potential for digital content and resources is huge, but the challenge to transition to these resources is very real for many teachers and schools (and districts and states) at this point.

Part of making personalized learning a reality is providing many different types of content along with multiple approaches to accessing that content. Some districts and schools strive for the UDL standard developed by CAST.[4]

UDL is an approach to content and assessment that ensures that all students will be able to access the content in a way that meets their learning needs. While the philosophy makes sense, the difficulties in making this approach a reality can often be overlooked due to the complexity and work required to do so.

Teachers are well aware that they can go on the Internet, search for a topic, and quickly have tens of thousands of possible resources. The challenge is that they could spend hours sifting through resources trying to find the perfect one. Many teachers appreciate portals or other learning management systems in which effective pieces of content have been identified for them to utilize for their lessons to meet the standards. Teachers can still amend or add resources, but it is helpful to have an in-depth digital curriculum, including a scope and sequence, from which they can build. This scope and sequence or curriculum may include all types of content (purchased and free), and ideally, this will allow students to have voice and choice, as well as provide options for teachers to meet the needs of all students. Few schools have yet to reach the point of having recommendation engines or generated playlists for students, but several are on their way. While teachers typically appreciate access to high-quality curated resources and content, it is important that the approach does not become prescriptive and limit the ownership and decision-making core to their teaching.

Unfortunately, too many times we have seen school leaders who are mesmerized by the "silver bullet" syndrome. School or district leaders—with a one-size-fits-all approach to their thinking about learning—purchase a program that all teachers must implement or a technology that all teachers must use without any regard for the learning outcomes being addressed. In one instance after a program was purchased, teachers spent countless hours learning to use the program, and students at all grade levels spent several hours every week engaging with the program. The expectation by the school leader was that there would be fidelity of implementation, and therefore, he would receive the results promised. The leader gave the teachers the training that they needed to understand the program's capabilities, and the teachers implemented the program with the prescribed fidelity, yet at the end of the semester, the results were not what they would have hoped. Committed to the program, the principal continued to stay the course and continued implementing the program the following year. At the end of the second year, many teachers applied for transfers. Ultimately, the school did not achieve the results it was hoping for because teachers were not able to engage with the content in a personal way. Much of their day was scripted, and they had little flexibility to change the pace or deviate from the script. They had little opportunity to teach. Schools that are successful and are models for others have strong leaders who involve stakeholders in creating and moving the vision of the school forward and allow teachers to personalize their classrooms to meet their own unique personalities as well as the needs of their students.

Some schools and districts are moving toward more personalized learning with playlists or other types of competency-based or personalized pathways, but they continue to engage the expertise of the teachers to implement and determine how to support students. New Classrooms has developed such algorithms and accompanying content for middle school math. Summit Public Schools have been able to move in the direction of a customized professional learning platform for teachers and students. Former principal Troy Moore's implementation of personalized pathways at Hawk Ridge Elementary School, while only somewhat digital, was driven by the use of data to drive progress and choice for students. These pathways provided opportunities for students to interact with content using different modalities and then show mastery of a concept through multiple learning styles. Students moved through the content at different pathways, creating a personalized pathway for each student.

Districts and schools that are effectively transitioning to personalized and digital learning are purposeful about how they approach content. Patapsco High School in Baltimore County, Maryland, led this work by having a group of science teachers develop their own interactive textbook for students who needed additional science to be prepared to enter the community college on grade level. The students who used this textbook may not have expected to go to college but now realized that they could if they could catch up on their science. This digital and somewhat personalized textbook allowed other teachers in the school to witness the pilot of the creation of rich digital content. This textbook provided an example of what was possible and allowed the teachers and coaches involved in its creation to become mentors to others.

Other districts, like Cabarrus County and Iredell-Statesville Schools in North Carolina, invite teachers who have the capacity and/or content knowledge to participate in a curriculum development workshop over the summer. Teachers are given a stipend to dedicate their time and expertise to develop digital content that teachers across the district can use. They are also taught some of the fundamentals of digital content creation and have peer-to-peer support throughout the process. Acknowledging that this creation process takes time, support, and expertise that teachers do not necessarily have in their everyday roles can go a long way to showing an understanding of the demands placed on teachers, especially in this transition.

It is equally important to continue to monitor and be on the lookout for content that you may want to purchase. Some states and districts purchase certain types of content or supplemental resources for schools to use, whereas others leave it up to the schools to make these decisions. Most schools use some type of purchased or subscription content, whether for instruction during the school day, for remediation, or for additional practice outside school. One of the biggest mistakes that schools (and districts) make is assuming people are using the products that they have. You, as the principal, have the opportunity to ask the provider or your district leader for usage data. Even more importantly, you can start to look for correlation between students and/or classes that use certain types of purchased (or other) content and outcomes. Determining this correlation may take more data and time than you have, but you can at least start by writing into the contract that usage data is required on a periodic (monthly or quarterly) basis. You can also ask questions about products used outside school in your survey or focus groups, and you can ask teachers what they need and like to use with students.

If you (or your district) provide a software product that teachers and students use, you should be careful to ensure that the subscription does not abruptly end without an explanation or a conversation with teachers. Teachers have to work hard to integrate programs effectively into their content and instruction. If they rely on certain resources, it's difficult for them start over with something else without solid evidence or data regarding its value, and it is especially difficult with no notice. This is an important aspect of sustainability, but also one that you can likely mitigate by having data to show the importance of the resource. Principal Amy Rickard shared an example in which her Morris Grove Elementary School teachers embraced and loved using a new product, Achieve 3000. However, the next year, after teachers had changed their instruction and lessons to incorporate Achieve 3000, the district no longer had the funding to pay for it. Experiences like this make teachers less willing to try the next time or the next thing. When you are engaging teachers in this transition, it is important to plan and be able to let teachers know that you will have access beyond a year and that you will work hard to develop strategies for continued funding for what is working.

The big takeaway with regard to content is that it—whether purchased, teacher developed, or OER—matters greatly to teachers and students. Content can support the transition to personalized and digital learning, or it can get in the way if teachers do not have a clear picture of their curriculum and if the content and curriculum do not support learning differences and personalized pathways. The development and curation of content are ongoing processes, but a careful plan in which teachers understand what is available and how to approach content in their instruction and lesson planning will be integral to your transition. If you have an instructional coach or a resource teacher in your building, have that person take the lead by spearheading the effort to help your teachers understand the resources available and how they can be utilized. The leader can help oversee the development of content or point people to resources that can help them. You might also want to consider partnering with nearby schools. You can tap into your district or other resources because sharing and borrowing what has been proven to work well will accelerate your transition.

DEVICES

Although you do not want to lead your transition to personalized and digital learning with devices or technology, sometimes you need to do so because funding is dedicated for this purpose at the beginning of your transition. In this case, you may be committing to devices before you have a chance to create a vision, understand student-centered teaching and learning, build a culture, and ensure professional learning is available. If this is the case, you may want to consider starting small—or starting with the teachers—and then remember to stop, develop that shared vision, and ask teachers to share strategies that are working as soon as possible.

If you are able to develop the shared vision first and ensure supports are in place, you should make a decision about devices based on what you want teaching and learning to look like. Some districts make a districtwide decision, whereas others allow schools to be involved in the decision. Some districts, like Mooresville Graded School District, decided that MacBooks made sense for grades three through twelve, whereas iPads were more appropriate for the younger grades. The key is that no one device is right or wrong as long as it meets the instructional needs of teachers and students. Following are some key questions you may want to consider:

- *Purpose.* What do we want students to be able to do with the devices? What are the primary purposes?
- *Portability and durability.* Is the device durable and portable enough for the students who will use it? Does it need to be portable?
- *Cloud or not.* Will students do most of their work on the Internet or in the cloud? Or will students be using software or programs on the computer itself?
- *Interface.* What interface will work best for the age of students?
- *Adaptability.* Will the device respond to and work for students with disabilities or learning differences? Are the options available on the device sufficient to work for the students' needs?
- *Four Cs and complexity of application.* Does the device support implementation and application of the Four Cs? Does the device allow students to create complex products and solutions?
- *Budget.* What is a realistic budget that allows you to ensure the other supports and resources are available when you have the devices (including professional learning, content, ongoing maintenance and replacement, and tools)?

The key is that districts and schools will have different answers to these questions, and even schools in the same district may have different needs. Some districts, like Horry County, South Carolina, have opted to incorporate a mix of devices, whereas Baltimore County, Maryland, has chosen a single type of laptop-tablet hybrid for all students and teachers. "Choosing the Right Digital Learning Device" is a helpful *Education Week* article, reminding us that this is about the learning and asking several key questions to consider.[5] Share this article with your technology leaders and ask stakeholders to read it before embarking on a discussion about what device or devices are best suited for your vision for teaching and learning.

If you do not have funding for devices at the school or district level, you may want to consider classroom sets, carts of devices, or a bring your own device (BYOD) model. Some districts may give you the option of what you would like to have.

Classroom sets provide opportunities for blended learning models or for students to use a device as needed in the classroom. A set could be desktop computers or five iPads or Chromebooks for the classroom. If teachers know that they have a certain number of devices, they can consistently plan to have them available, and students will become accustomed to using them seamlessly in the classroom. Teachers may also have students work in small groups or pairs, with each group of partners having a device to use, record their work, or create a product.

A cart with devices may be used in conjunction with smaller classroom sets for times when a teacher wants every student or more of the students to have a device available. Classroom carts should be equipped to keep the devices charged and should also be designed for ease of checking devices in and out. Because schools that go this route tend to have only a few carts of classroom sets or maybe one per grade level or content area, teachers have to plan ahead and check out the carts to use on a particular day. This approach is certainly possible but allows teachers to get out of the habit of using the technology. In other cases, some teachers tend to hold onto the carts and use them all the time, thus creating a divide in the school.

Bring your own device is an approach that some schools or districts are using to maximize the devices that students already own. This model frees up resources to invest more money at the school or district level in broadband or digital content to support the transition. BYOD can evoke a great deal of fear among teachers because they wonder how they are to manage a classroom with many different devices, platforms, and tools. Parents, teachers, and leaders often worry about equity and students who do not have access to a device that they can bring to school and use beyond the school day. These are critical points for principals and stakeholders to consider, but several schools have shown that going this route can work for students and teachers and advance personalized and digital learning. Typically, the BYOD approach leads to using applications that are based in the cloud. Students might use Google Apps or another learning management system or other programs that can be accessed from any device, usually including smartphones, laptops, or tablets. Protections or filters can still be implemented on the school network itself to help alleviate some concerns while students are in school, but addressing digital citizenship is critical with BYOD.

Brier Creek Elementary is one of almost thirty schools in Wake County, North Carolina, that has volunteered to be a part of a BYOD initiative. This effort has involved extensive professional learning for teachers and school leaders, but overall schools decided to tackle their need for more digital learning by tapping into the resources that their students have already. Former principal Sandy Chambers focused on teaching and learning, and she used some school-purchased devices to supplement what students had from home. She also addressed some instructional needs that may have been better served on a tablet or another device. At Brier Creek, students collaborate, create products, and think critically, and the technology is a tool to help them accomplish their work in different ways.

One critical aspect of Brier Creek's approach has been a strong collaborative approach among the teachers. The school started a blog for teachers to share what they are doing with the BYOD efforts and how they integrate technology and digital learning to improve instruction. This informal sharing has allowed some teachers to quickly emerge as leaders, while also giving those more reluctant or nervous teachers support and ideas to consider. The *BCES Revolutionizing Education* blog shares real stories from real teachers and allows other teachers, parents, students, and the community to see what is happening in their school.[6] The technology and the BYOD model are not at the forefront; the teaching and learning are. You can view this blog and even join the community to follow their work. This excellent example of job-embedded professional learning often leads to collaboration and visits among teachers to continue their growth.

It is important to reiterate the bottom line with regard to devices: One right answer does not exist, and you may have several best options for your school depending on your answers to the key questions shared previously. You may want to visit schools to see different ways that tools and devices are being used, and you should consider focus groups and discussions with experts to support your decisions. Your technology leaders, coaches, teachers, and students will help you consider and test what is best for your school and students.

DATA AND ASSESSMENT SYSTEMS

Technology provides many additional avenues for using assessments and then using data from assessments and other sources to personalize learning for students. Using data can fall under the umbrella of learning analytics. More formally, the Society for Learning Analytics Research (SoLAR) defines learning analytics as "the measurement, collection, analysis and reporting of data about learners and their contexts, for purposes of understanding and optimizing learning and the environments in which it occurs."[7] While you may not dive into the nitty-gritty of learning analytics, you will be employing it if you can understand how to collect, share, and analyze data that allows you to personalize learning for students. Using data and learning analytics is critical for personalizing learning for all students and leading to stronger retention and achievement outcomes. The improvements in access to data and variety of assessments and other pertinent information have dramatically changed the education landscape.[8]

Much more is possible, but this is unlikely to translate into a simple "plug and play" option for your teachers and students unless your district or school has developed or worked with a company to design a robust system with a dashboard that meets the needs of teachers, students, and parents. As you make decisions about programs and systems to purchase or use, you must think about your goals for supporting teachers and students with the assessments and data they need to make instructional decisions and promote personalized pathways. Your district may provide you with benchmark assessments and other tools to assess students, as well as ways to access the data.

Having the right tools is one important component, but if you do not have a culture in which teachers are comfortable that the data is used to support instruction and not to penalize, they are unlikely to embrace using data as a core to their practice. The Alliance for Excellent Education explains that educators should not fear ramifications for using data and taking risks in implementing strategies based on that data, along with assessments and other information available. Leaders should encourage educators to utilize data and take risks. This will change the culture to one in which data is not only used but valued.[9] You have a significant role in helping teachers understand and see the value of data and assessment beyond evaluative and punitive uses.

One way to consider assessments is to ensure that they are "for learning" rather than "of learning."[10] Many educators have written and spoken about this concept, but having your teachers think about this distinction can go a long way to understanding how to use data and assessment to personalize learning. When teachers give students a test, especially a multiple-choice test, take a week or two to grade it and give it back to the students, and then do not provide any opportunities for the students to learn what they missed or to reflect on the assessment, they are very much using assessment "of learning." Imagine instead that they provide students with performance activities to complete based on where they are in their learning and then provide feedback via a rubric or another means almost immediately, along with the opportunity to improve on the areas in which students did not reach mastery. This is assessment "for learning" because the purpose is to understand where students are and how to help them achieve the standards. While this example may provide two extremes on the assessment spectrum, teachers can support student growth and help students see assessments as part of their learning in many ways. Doing so helps support the growth mindset and the idea that failure is acceptable as long as the students try again.

Your teachers may choose to use freely available tools for formative assessment, such as Kahoot or Socrative. These tools allow students to assess the class in an interactive way without embarrassing anyone for not knowing the information. Because teachers share the correct answer, students know immediately whether they got the question correct rather than waiting for days or assuming they knew the information. Additionally, the teachers can download the results to use immediately.

Another possible use of technology to support personalized learning is a digital portfolio. While the concept of portfolios is not new, digital learning today allows us to do much more with the student artifacts, including sharing them with parents digitally, allowing for curation over the years, and providing a basis for moving to microcredentials or digital badging because the process for submitting artifacts already exists. Eventually, this portfolio could include a multitude of artifacts, including those from informal learning or extracurricular activities. Keeping these artifacts over time, especially with the feedback via a rubric or another approach, helps build sustainability for the efforts and allows students, teachers, and parents to see student progress over time.

Former principal Tim Lauer shared how Meriwether Lewis Elementary School took advantage of Google Apps to have a more competency-based, personalized approach. A teacher dashboard tool allowed teachers to have access to student work in an ongoing way, and teachers could provide feedback in real time to students. Tim commented,

We're a Google Apps school. We are Chromebooks one-to-one in second through fifth grades. One of the tools that the teachers have latched onto is Hapara, the teacher dashboard. It's an interface to the Google Apps environment. Everything students create is automatically shared—journal writing, slide show, essay—in the drive, and they can see it and interact with it in the classroom. The teachers are doing this on a consistent basis and have made it part of the workflow. There are some interactive places to see what kids have done and management tools to remind them if they are somewhere they shouldn't be. We approach it in a helpful reminder way, like the manual version. That has really allowed teachers to be more thoughtful in their feedback, using commenting in Google Apps. There is an aspect of blended learning that has evolved, even though it wasn't planned. Teachers will say, "I'll be on at 7," and if students are working, and have questions, they'll be there. You have to be careful not to force, but most of the teachers do work at home, and they see the benefit of this.

Overall, teachers see value in using technology for assessments, but many share that the abundance of data almost makes it unmanageable to use on a regular basis. Teachers can be swimming in data, and many have not been taught how to read or synthesize the data and, more importantly, how to apply it. You have the opportunity to support teachers and your staff in using data to improve and personalize instruction in the following ways:

- *Ensuring that data is actionable.* You need to make sure that teachers are able to isolate data that is useful and actionable. Ideally, this will be through a platform or dashboard that allows teachers to see the critical data without the noise of every possible piece of information. Your district may provide this, but you may need to be persistent with your district leaders if the data is not useful for your efforts to personalize learning. Consider how to provide access to or collect data that is not strictly achievement data. This could include information about learning differences, including executive function, working memory, or motivation, or social emotional learning aspects. The more the data available includes the many facets of information that support personalized learning, the more likely it is that teachers can truly meet the needs of each student. The key is that teachers are not wasting hours and hours sifting through data that will not support their work.

- *Helping teachers learn how to use data.* Teachers are often afraid of data. They may be afraid of what it will show about their teaching, and they may not be confident in their ability to understand and interpret the data. You can help guide them through a process of using data. Invite a district leader to work with the teachers or provide a workshop that models how to look at data. Some principals choose to have data meetings with a team or individual teachers to look at data together. You cannot do this every week for every teacher, but it may give you a chance to look at data with them while modeling how they should consider, interpret, and then develop action steps based on the information. You may want to help teachers focus on a particular area at a time, or you may ask them to begin to use some of their assessment data from ongoing and performance-based assessments in conjunction with the district- or school-provided ones. You may even want to work with teachers on the data of one or two students first, especially for a student who is struggling and for whom the teacher is trying to better understand how to help. Teachers may want to explore additional learning opportunities, including through microcredentials, to understand how to use data and then apply it with a student. Once teachers begin to use data and see that it helps them personalize learning and understand their students, the process will become second nature to them.

- *Carving out time.* As with professional learning overall, teachers will need time to dig into, discuss, and begin to use data to personalize learning. Help your teams think about how often they might like to carve out time to look and discuss data. Provide them with strategies for their professional learning communities (PLCs) to study data for a student together and then work independently or to work in pairs or the whole team if teachers share many students. Help them see the connections to the work of the school toward the shared vision so that this data analysis does not become just one more thing they have to do. If teachers don't see value in the exercise of using alternative assessments and analyzing data, they will complete only the perfunctory tasks without developing sustainable approaches in their practice.

DIGITAL CITIZENSHIP

You likely will hear immediately from at least a subset of parents or community members that digital learning will expose students to things they should not see or read or things that will put students at risk because of others on the

Internet. These parents who want to hinder the use of technology in schools often lack an understanding of how digital technology is used for learning, and they have a concern about the unknown. Other parents report that they already have to fight to keep their children off "screens," and they do not want their children to have more time on screen at school. According to Project Tomorrow, helping parents understand and support a transition to a different sort of learning is a big concern among many administrators. "The top challenge reported by principals who have implemented blended learning include: educating parents on their role in supporting blended learning for their child (61 percent)."[11]

Teachers may also express fear of what to do if a student happens on or seeks out something inappropriate while online in school or while on a school-owned device. Many districts and schools rush to filter out every possible danger by prohibiting students and teachers from accessing certain sites on the school network, such as YouTube, Twitter, or Facebook. Blocking access becomes a slippery slope. Putting child protections in place certainly makes sense, but filtering all content may not be the best course of action for the students. Many of the students have access to the Internet outside of school or on devices other than those provided. Even in schools with high poverty, a majority of students have smartphones or other access to the Internet. "[E]ight in 10 high school students reported owning a smartphone. The number of students using smartphones in class increased from 44 percent to 53 percent [in one year, 2014–2015]."[12]

An important component of the systems and structures to have in place is a robust approach to digital citizenship. The idea of digital citizenship is to help students, teachers, and other stakeholders develop the skills and understanding to use technology and the Internet safely and appropriately. One argument against filtering extensively is that district leaders, principals, coaches, and teachers would prefer to help students learn how to be good digital citizens and to use technology responsibly. Students need to learn how to act and what to do when they are not at school or on a school-owned device.

A combined approach of some child safety precautions and perhaps some filtering, along with a focus on digital citizenship, can be very successful, yet many principals can share stories of how a student saw something that should not have been seen. This is not the norm, and it is not pervasive, but it is a reality that you should be prepared to address. If you have your school code of conduct in place, with expectations for proper behavior clearly laid out, and if you have helped teachers be prepared, you can address this issue seriously and swiftly so that other teachers, students, and parents understand that irresponsible online behavior will not be tolerated.

Digital citizenship not only includes safety and appropriateness but also addresses ownership and appropriate attribution for content found on the Internet. Teachers who already address citations and topics like APA and MLA style of references are poised to address how this issue is similar and different on the Internet. Open education resources, like EasyBib, Citation Machine, and BibMe, can also help students ensure that they are providing the proper credit in the right format.

Many tools can help protect students, and many online resources are available to support the development of a digital citizenship program in your school. One of the most frequently used programs is from Common Sense Media.[13] It provides a way to think about digital citizenship at different grade levels and ages, while providing a comprehensive approach to empower students as they use the Internet and technology. Another good resource is KidSmartz because it has tips for teachers and parents as well as interactive activities for students.[14]

One key point to remember and share with your teachers is that digital citizenship cannot be taught in a day or a week. Students will make mistakes, and they will go places and do things they should not be doing. Learning to be a responsible digital citizen is an ongoing process and should be referenced and addressed frequently. For this reason, you will want an overall scope and sequence to ensure that the comprehensive topic is covered while also providing teachers with tools and resources to use in an ongoing way.

Parents can be very helpful in reinforcing the tenets of digital citizenship by understanding what students are learning and also by knowing what questions to ask and what to look for in terms of their children's interactions online. Be honest and up front with parents without scaring them with only the extreme stories. Having a parent night or dedicating a PTA/PTO program to educate parents is a great way to help them understand how to support and be involved with their children both at home and in school. Also as part of the parent education, share the products or other work that students are developing that are enhanced or made possible by the digital learning opportunities. Once parents see the possibilities and how digital learning provides a more personalized approach, empowers students, and addresses the Four Cs, they will be more open to understanding why the digital learning is important and how we can help our students become digitally literate. Consistent with engaging stakeholders in the development and implementation of personalized and digital learning, you will want to ensure that stakeholders see themselves as a part of the digital citizenship effort. This is an important place to show students that you trust them, but with that trust comes a responsibility to embody digital citizenship each day.

FUNDING FOR SUSTAINABILITY AND PARTNERING WITH YOUR DISTRICT

Depending on your district or your status as a public, charter, or private school, the responsibility and opportunity for developing a digital sustainability plan may or may not rest on you. For some, districts provide a robust infrastructure, access, devices, data and assessment tools, and a digital citizenship curriculum to support schools. For others, the district may not be as ready as a principal like you might be, or you may be in a school where developing this plan is not part of your role. We have all heard of personalized and digital learning efforts that lead with the device or the technology, including a significant purchase, yet do not have an implementation or a sustainability plan. One district leader who received significant funding but could not really articulate where the district was going in integrating digital learning went so far as to call the funding they had received "magic money." He further shared that they didn't know when the money was coming, and they didn't know when or if it would come again. As in any business, the technology and digital learning supports needed for personalized learning must have an ongoing budget and a plan for replacing and keeping the technologies in working order.

Having technicians who can fix things or set up new technologies for students and teachers is important, and you must not allow your coaches or media coordinators to fall into the habit of spending most of their time putting out fires with technology glitches. Having the technicians and the instructional technology facilitators, coaches, or media coordinators in place to support teachers and students is an important part of your sustainability plan, but you must also have a plan to ensure that you can replace and expand on the technologies as needed. Some describe broadband access and other technology expenses like utilities. We budget in our homes and schools for electricity, heat, and phones. With the transition to personalized and digital learning, and truly almost anywhere today, broadband access is a utility. The Consortium for School Networking (CoSN) is the association that represents technology leaders in schools and districts. It recently updated its Total Cost of Ownership tool, which helps define what it really costs to maintain and sustain technology.[15] Those costs are important to know and to keep in mind when budgeting.

While you can have the best intentions with a budget and a sustainability plan, many schools continue to rely on the PTA or one-time grant funding to support technology. That approach may be an effective part of your sustainability plan, especially if you ensure that the one-time funding provides what your teachers and students need to improve instruction rather than simply what someone feels like giving at the time. However, you will also want to work with your district or with your finance person to develop a funding stream like you would for library content, operations costs, instructional materials, and human capacity needs. You can begin to think differently about resources to free up money to use for technology, whether using textbook money for digital content, rethinking how you use your team members to support the transition, or considering efficiencies that you may be able to accomplish with the addition of more technologies. ERStrategies is an organization that focuses on helping districts and schools think strategically about resources and budgets. It offers a budget simulation tool, School Budget Hold'em, that allows you to plug in your real numbers.[16] This tool may be more effective for you to share or complete with your district, but it does support diving into budgets if this is an area over which you have some control. ERStrategies also provides other tools that address different areas discussed throughout this chapter and book.[17]

TRY IT TOMORROW

1. **Meet with your administrative team or teacher leaders to make a plan for addressing digital citizenship at your school.** You might want to consider including the media coordinator and an instructional coach or others who support teachers in these conversations. With this team, create a plan that ensures teachers understand why this is important and that they have the support and resources needed to integrate the digital citizenship themes into

their curriculum. Several groups have published content for teachers and students around digital citizenship. Common Sense Media, in particular, has focused on helping students, teachers, and administrators understand how to ensure that students have the skills and mindset that they need to be safe and act appropriately online. This includes a scope and sequence for students, professional development, and a certification program.

2. **Do a quick survey of teachers, students, and parents about their access to technology and the Internet.** For teachers, focus on what's happening in school while leading lessons. Ask if filters are getting in their way of utilizing strong content that would facilitate learning (such as YouTube for OER materials). For students, get more information about their perceptions about technology use in school, access to the Internet and adequate bandwidth at school and at home, and any places that they are able to access the Internet (for example, Starbucks or McDonald's). Ask parents about students' access to devices and the Internet and whether they would be interested in programs with reduced rates. This is especially important for low-income students who are eligible for free or reduced lunch. If you are not sure about using a survey, you could hold focus groups with each of these groups or even individual discussions with a representative sample. The important thing is that you do not assume that you know what access people have or do not have or how the Internet and devices available are working for teachers.

Once you have this data, especially if you identify needs, set up a meeting with your district office's chief technology officer to discuss your plans for digital transition. During the conversation, make sure to discuss strengths and needs identified for technology and bandwidth and ask about the capacity of your current infrastructure to support your future plans.

8

Build Human Capacity
with Teams

Always choose people over systems.
The process and system can be replaced if
needed, but great people are invaluable.

—MICHAEL ARMSTRONG

Many of the chapters in this book focus specifically on people. Even those chapters that address the vision or the systems needed for personalized and digital learning stress that all these things depend significantly on human capacity. The principals interviewed for this book shared great advice that validated what we often hear from district and school leaders across the country—that so much of this work comes down to *people*. Here, we examine the important issues surrounding people—recruiting, retaining, and empowering the educators in your building. Through an understanding of the many roles available to teachers, principals have opportunities to consider strategic staffing, team teaching, and hybrid roles for educators to increase effectiveness, mentoring, and teacher retention. Your ability to build and sustain a strong team that is ready and willing to move forward in the journey toward personalized and digital learning can make or break your effectiveness in this transition.

MAXIMIZE YOUR TEAM, RECRUIT WELL, AND RETAIN EXCELLENT TEACHERS

Cultivating a team that has the necessary skills and knowledge to excel in their roles, as well as the ability and drive to improve and continue their own learning, is a critical role of school leaders. Between 40 and 50 percent of teachers leave the profession within the first five years of their career, and many note a lack of administrative support and being isolated.[1] Those who stay feel the increased demands on and criticisms of teachers. This awareness can contribute to an overall negative morale. Many new teachers feel unprepared for the complexities of the job when they begin teaching. They often feel the job is not what they had envisioned—it's more about testing, paperwork, and meetings and less about helping children learn. Changing roles within a school can create personnel challenges. It sometimes happens that excellent classroom teachers get tapped for coaching roles, yet they do not have a deep understanding of adult learning or how to effectively guide and coach educators. Bringing out the best in your staff can be challenging and complex.

If you're an incoming principal, you will undoubtedly inherit a staff. You will have only a little say about who your teachers, coaches, and other staff members in the building are. When this is the case, you will need to consider the following issues:

- how best to utilize the staff you have currently
- how to ensure that those who are not effective have either support to improve and grow or a pathway to a different role
- how to maximize the potential of the team members that you do get to recruit and hire

Maximize Your Team

Whether you are a new principal or a seasoned principal at a new—to you—school, take the time to meet individually with each teacher and staff member. During the course of your conversations, try to understand what they see as working well in the school, in their grade level, and in their classroom. Ask them what they want to improve in those same areas. Pay special attention to what drives or motivates them to do what they do each day; figure out what is their *why*. These conversations will go a long way toward showing them that you care about what they think and that you value their thoughts on the school and the direction it is going. If you have been leading a school for a few years, you may decide you want to continue this discussion process. While it can be time consuming, you may be able to alleviate a great deal of the noise and confusion that can swirl around by meeting directly to talk not about the teacher's evaluation, but rather the school and teaching and learning.

Research shows, and our work with school districts around the country confirms, that teachers are interested in pursuing hybrid roles in which they continue to teach in the classroom while also having additional roles in the school.[2] These roles may include mentoring beginning or struggling teachers; developing content or curriculum; or piloting something specific to the transition to personalized and digital learning, such as the use of a learning management system, student-led conferences, or a one-to-one initiative in their classroom. If you decide to ask teachers to take on a hybrid role, make sure that you take something off their plate at the same time. Perhaps you can have them teach one or two fewer sections of a class or maybe take away some of the more administrative duties that someone else can readily cover. Shifting and balancing roles and responsibilities can be challenging but well worth the time and energy you devote to it.

This focus on maximizing your staff should also include supporting teacher assistants, or others who support teachers and students, in taking on additional roles. For example, Michael Armstrong, former principal of Bugg Creative Arts Magnet School, developed an additional "special" in his elementary school focused on STEM. Often in elementary schools, students don't have opportunities to spend sufficient time on science or social studies and, therefore, may not get to explore labs or other related topics—especially integrating the Four Cs. By establishing this additional special block, Michael was able to creatively staff the STEM lab, while also freeing up classroom teachers so that they had double blocks for planning, PLC meetings, and professional development. He used funding pulled together from some additional months of teacher assistant positions. This arrangement benefited the students in that the approach was more personalized and often integrated hands-on, student-centered methods. Teachers also had enough time, beyond the frequently used twenty-two or thirty-minute blocks, to dive in and accomplish real work, together and independently.

Troy Moore, former principal of Hawk Ridge Elementary School, participated in an effort called the Opportunity Culture, developed by Public Impact, to creatively use his staff members.[3] This program provided Troy the flexibility to redesign the role of his teachers and to provide additional pay for those taking on the mentoring and coaching of other teachers. It also enabled him to provide additional support for those who stayed in classroom teaching roles. As a result of the redesign, some classes ended up having more students, but the teachers of those classes had more opportunities for coteaching and coplanning. One key aspect of the Opportunity Culture work is that every adult is directly responsible for students in the building, so a mentor/coach is directly responsible for the students of all the teachers with whom that coach works. Participating in Opportunity Culture gave master teachers the opportunity to grow while still being directly connected to and responsible for students. The program also provided all of Troy's teachers with additional support and coaching. He said,

> During the last year of my leadership at Hawk Ridge, I was able to dig into the work of Opportunity Culture and identify teacher leaders to lead multiple classrooms. This work uses various models to slightly decrease actual staff but use the money allocation to further incentivize those amazing teacher leaders to look beyond their four walls and take ownership of far more than their normal twenty-five students. I saw it as an opportunity [to] reward and get these teacher leaders exposed to more students and their colleagues.

Some of the master teachers may have opted to pursue roles in administration if they had not had this opportunity because in most schools teachers ready to move beyond the classroom have very limited options. Additionally, the teachers, parents, and students could clearly see that this transition to personalized pathways was happening and that the school was willing to invest differently in the human capital needed to make it happen.

While you may not have the opportunity to pursue the formal Opportunity Culture program in your school, you may be able to creatively utilize your district's structure to create new roles within your existing budget. In this situation, the following idea from Rear Admiral Grace Hopper, a pioneering computer scientist before technology was pervasive, becomes real: "The most dangerous phrase in the language is 'we've always done it that way.'" Creative thinking can lead to some potentially great new ideas about staffing and teacher roles.

At New Tech West High School, former principal Erin Frew creatively paired or grouped teachers to accelerate the transition to more project-based learning with a cross-curricular approach. Making this process a priority spoke volumes to the teachers, and they were able to draw on each other's strengths in the planning and implementation of this student-centered personalized and digital learning. Erin also gave team leaders new, specific roles:

> There is a lead teacher on each of the teams. That lead teacher provides technical assistance for those who struggle. For example, on the electives team, there were a couple of less tech-savvy teachers, but the one who is more tech savvy encourages and works with them. On another team, there were two brand new teachers. The more experienced teachers provide some mentoring to the new teachers to make sure they were implementing with fidelity.

While some teachers may be willing to support or mentor other teachers, they may not be comfortable simply asserting themselves in that role. Also, some teachers who need help or technical assistance may not be willing to ask. When you purposefully assign and discuss the roles, both the mentor and the mentees now have a specific way to help or be helped.

Don't be afraid to be creative and truly think about how you utilize individual talents to serve the vision of your school and to impact the students and teachers most effectively. Once you think through what is possible and, ideally, engage teachers—and even students and parents—in that discussion, ask lots of "what if" questions and see what your possibilities are within the parameters that exist. Troy had a teacher assistant serving in the role of an instructional technology facilitator because she was the most qualified for that role, even though she did not have the credentials for the title. Michael created a dean of academics and a dean of professional learning even though those titles did not formally exist in his district or state.

While you might be limited by pay structures and the overall budget, you may be able to do more within the structures that exist than you ever imagined simply by asking, "What do we need? What makes sense?" Garner input and be transparent with your thinking and decision making, and be willing to explain your decisions to your stakeholders. If they truly support the vision you all share for your school, and they support your students and teachers, your decisions and actions will help teachers find roles that can be transformative for your school.

When John Bernia, former principal of Carleton Middle School, began to look at his faculty and staff differently, he recognized that he could not lead the transformation of his school alone. He sums up well how he approached maximizing the team in his middle school:

> As a leader, [I believe] my role isn't to be the one with all the answers. My call is to create the space and time for our staff to learn, to connect people with colleagues that can help them, to ask quality questions, and to ensure our teachers have what they need to incorporate instructional technology into their practice. Classroom teachers who are "doing the work" in their classrooms have far better command on what works and what doesn't in classrooms. I have to listen, encourage, observe, ask, and support.

Recruit Well

While you may inherit a team of teachers and have only limited opportunities to hire new faculty and staff, you should ensure that you take full advantage of each opportunity to bring someone new into your school. Even the turnover and/or addition of one or two people can be an important catalyst in the transition to personalized and digital learning. New team members can also lead a shift away from negative culture, or they can ask questions that others have been afraid to ask. Tim Lauer, former principal of Meriwether Lewis Elementary School, shares how he maximized the impact of new hires:

> I think in terms of getting the right people on board, in terms of employees, I've been able to make a few hires that have given us a lot of traction. It's about getting the right people there who interact with each other. We brought on four staff in the last three to four years. Separately, they are great teachers and people; but in addition, they are great at collaboration and sharing their work. We've gotten to a point where we have nineteen teachers sharing on Twitter every day. Tweeting points out there's something good about Mr. Hanson's math activity, but then another teacher sees that, which leads to further conversation and a whole level of engagement that wouldn't be there just walking down the hall and saying hi to each other. It's tough to connect when you're isolated in your room. With getting the right people on board, you have a whole mix of people talking. Those who might wait and hold back now have someone to show the way. This year things have gotten real traction—and technology has been key.

Superintendent Suzanne Lacey needed to create new roles at the district and school levels in Talladega County to directly support the transition to digital and project-based learning:

> I think what I would like others to know is that as you grow, you have to have more manpower. No one has enough, but through this process we have been able to add the digital learning specialist piece. It's so important. We created the coordinator for instructional technology. I had to have someone at this level lead this through the district. The infrastructure and technology had to grow as well. That is sometimes challenging to build into your budget, but as you go through the process for doing great things for kids, that sometimes means you need additional manpower to work through it. It's a good problem. These digital learning specialists have emerged as experts. They didn't set about to do that, but it's a beautiful metamorphosis. It's the fun and challenging part—to take talent and create roles to lead the vision. It's a growing pain. You are going to have growing pains.

Whether you're creating a new role or filling a vacated role, you should make sure you are prepared to make the most of the opportunity. You may be urgently trying to fill a hard-to-fill spot, but if you have in place a process that is designed to ensure that new hires will buy into and be prepared for your vision, you are more likely to make an effective choice. Principals often ask us how they will know whether a teacher will be prepared to jump in and accelerate the transition to personalized and digital learning. Teachers do not typically come to a potential job with an add-on certification for digital learning. Many current principals we work with share that while the teachers may be comfortable using the technology, tools, and social media, they have not been taught nor have they practiced how to effectively integrate it into their pedagogy. Some more veteran teachers may have more specific experience with personalized and digital learning, and you will want to make sure that you dive into this issue specifically during the recruitment and interview process. You may also begin to see or hear about trends in terms of which universities or which districts have provided more extensive support and learning around personalized and digital learning. Talk to principals in your district and in your state. Use our *#LeadingPDL* to ask questions of your fellow principals.

Erin included a performance-based aspect in her interview process. She asked top candidates to prepare and lead a lesson with a real class at her school that was directly tied to the standards and their work. By giving a teacher candidate only broad direction, she was able to quickly see his creativity, whether he would build in personalized options and learning agency, and whether he was comfortable utilizing technology to strengthen the lesson. She could also ask reflection questions after the lesson to see if the teacher learned from the experience and was willing to be vulnerable and talk about what went well and what might warrant improvement.

Few things can showcase a teacher's ability to teach than teaching. When using this performance-based approach, ask follow-up questions about other examples of lessons the teacher has, what she might do the next day or few days, and how she would carry this lesson through on an ongoing basis. Asking these questions helps ensure that the lesson the candidate taught for you is indicative of day-to-day practice, not just a one-time deal.

Include learning walks as a part of the interview process with a group of candidates or with an individual candidate. Include a couple of teachers from your school in this activity. This approach allows you to hear what the candidate picks up on and believes, while also seeing his willingness to collaborate and discuss with others. This walk will also give the teacher candidate a chance to consider whether he wants and is willing to be a part of a school in which this type of learning and collaboration is encouraged and is part of each day. You want people who want to work in this way, so if candidates become disinterested in your school because you asked them to participate in some of the regular happenings, you are probably fortunate to discover this issue before they are part of the team.

You can help build an effective staff for personalized and digital learning by understanding the competencies you want and need teachers to have and directing interviews toward those competencies. Especially consider some of the key points around technology not being on the side or an add-on, but rather directly part of the planning for instruction. Understand potential staff members' philosophy on teaching and learning, and whether they have a lens toward personalized learning and understanding learning differences; or if they tend to expect all students to learn the same way at the same time. While the extreme is unlikely to emerge in an interview, you can ask certain questions or include other aspects of the interview process to garner more information about candidates.

Consider using some key interview questions that dive more deeply into your vision for personalized and digital learning. They are helpful in your thinking about how teacher candidates will augment or hinder the culture you are building. Following are some questions that might be helpful with teaching roles:

- How have you approached personalized learning in your student teaching or teaching experience?
- How would a student describe your classroom and instruction?
- How do you build your curriculum and instruction to be personalized?
- Describe a time when you sought to utilize technology and digital learning and it supported student learning effectively.
- Describe a time when using digital learning did not go well. What did you do?
- Describe a situation in which you worked with another teacher or teachers to develop a lesson.
- How would you design the ideal classroom or learning environment (physical space)?
- How would you hope that a coach might work with you?
- How would you feel about teachers visiting your classroom to learn from you and your teaching?
- If you want to learn something new to improve your teaching, how would you go about doing that?
- Describe a time when you disagreed with someone and worked through that disagreement to reach your collective goal.

These questions are not the only ones that can aid you in your search, but they do give you an idea of how to dig a little further and see whether teacher candidates will want to do things in a way that supports your vision and if they are willing to take risks, work collaboratively, and be vulnerable in working with others.

Similarly, you need to be targeted in your questions for the roles of instructional coach, media coordinator, or even district-level instructional technology specialist. Following are some questions that might be helpful with these teaching roles:

- How would you describe personalized learning?

- Share an example of what personalized learning looked like in your classroom or in a classroom of a teacher with whom you worked.
- How would you like students to describe your school?
- What is your vision for coaching? How would you hope that vision could work with teachers? With administrators? With others in the building?
- How would you approach a teacher who was resistant to working with you?
- How would you approach a teacher who was resistant to trying new things with digital learning?
- How do you assess where a teacher is or what a teacher needs?
- How do you build your curriculum and instruction to be personalized?
- Describe a time when you sought to utilize technology and digital learning and it supported student learning effectively.
- Describe a time when using digital learning did not go well. What did you do?
- How would you design the ideal classroom or learning environment (physical space)? How might you approach the media center or common areas in the school?
- Describe a time when you disagreed with someone and worked through that disagreement to reach your collective goal.
- If you want to learn something new to improve your coaching, how would you go about doing that?

This interview process is not something you should do alone. Involve other teachers to get multiple perspectives. Involve students and get feedback from them about how they feel teacher candidates would blend into the school culture and the teaching team. Everyone's investment in this hiring process is critical, especially in this transition to personalized and digital learning, which requires an effective, collaborative culture.

Retain Excellent Team Members

Teacher retention and staff turnover can be big problems, especially in certain geographical and content areas. You need to be thoughtful as you develop new roles and hire new team members, but this process can never be at the expense of honoring and retaining excellent teachers, coaches, and administrators. You may feel as though you have limited financial incentives for your current team members because it is unlikely that you can give raises or bonuses outside of prescriptive parameters. However, research shows that teachers do not typically leave because of low pay, although some states have made decisions, often legislative ones, that seem almost antiteacher, and salary may play a bigger role than normal. Teachers care about their working conditions and their ability to have an impact on students. If teachers feel they are supported, have a voice, and believe they are part of a team with a leader who is working toward a vision focused on students, they are much more likely to stay in their current positions and in their schools. According to Linda Darling-Hammond, president of the Learning Policy Institute, "Working conditions are even more important for keeping people in once they've made the choice to teach. . . . Teachers who are well prepared leave at more than two times lower rates than teachers who are not fully prepared."[4]

Teachers stay because they like what they do and where they do it. But they also stay when they feel they are doing a good job. The first year of the transition to personalized and digital learning can feel like a teacher's first year of teaching ever, which can destabilize even a seasoned veteran teacher. When teachers leave the tried and true of what they know and jump into the unknown, this process is exhausting and frustrating. If teachers feel supported by their colleagues and their school leaders during the process, they gain confidence. Once teachers are over the hurdle of taking the initial risks and making big changes, they will want to remain part of the school community if they can see that what they are doing and their instruction are helping students succeed. Many teachers who are deeply embedded in personalized and digital learning will tell you that they could not go back to traditional classroom instruction. Often they are also the teachers who opt to continue teaching even when they could retire. These teachers become hooked on being able to teach in a way that is consistent with their beliefs, and they find successes in the classroom that reinforce the reasons they entered the profession in the first place.

Recognizing and honoring people's strengths can also contribute to job satisfaction and retention. The opening section of this chapter focused on developing hybrid roles and ensuring that you are maximizing the people you have. Interestingly, providing these types of added opportunities, especially to teachers who struggled with a desire to step out of the classroom but saw the only option as classroom teaching or administration, can go a long way to retaining excellent educators. Let teachers know that you are willing to work with them and be creative to provide them with opportunities to grow.

On the flip side, be willing to help people who are not suited for the shared vision and the transition to personalized and digital learning find other opportunities or jobs. While you want to retain the excellent teachers who are trying new things and making an effort to learn and grow with a constant focus on what is best for students, you do not want to continue the effort with teachers who are simply not willing to try or to grow. If you have tried taking these teachers on site visits to see in action what personalized and digital learning could look like and you've had a coach or other teachers work with them to try new strategies in a safe space, and you continue to get resistance, you may need to begin having conversations and document more formally a lack of effort and willingness to be a part of the team and vision. Many principals find that when the school has a shared vision and almost all the teachers, students, and parents are clearly moving in that direction, some teachers will make their own decision to leave if they have another option. You need to let teachers know from the beginning that not trying or not embracing the vision is not an option. However, you will provide every structure, support, and learning opportunity possible if they are willing to put themselves out there and take risks for the betterment of instruction.

We mention developing an effective culture early and often because it is at the core of what is needed to truly transition to personalized and digital learning. Part of this culture is the engagement of stakeholders and an environment in which people are willing and trust that they can take risks and try new things. Building a culture that encourages and allows people to grow without fear helps provide the support that contributes to retention. What holds the culture together is a shared vision in which everyone is moving in the same direction, even if at different paces and in different ways. Maintaining this vision will help you quickly discern which teachers are with you; you must ensure they understand that they are valued and have options to stay and grow. Principal Amy Rickard of Morris Grove Elementary School shares, "One of my [graduate school professors] who was a teacher, principal, and superintendent, said 'Leaders always push people up, make people better.'"

CONNECT AND GROW

Maximizing your team and recruiting and retaining excellent teachers will go a long way toward supporting your vision and your work within the school, but those two things are not enough. We challenge you to remember that while looking after and encouraging all the people in your school to build their capacity, you should not forget to take care of yourself—personally and professionally. It is your responsibility to nurture your own path and progress. While you may attend principal meetings at your district, it is unlikely that this effort will be enough. Often those meetings become focused more on addressing compliance or requirements and less on growing yourself as a leader for personalized and digital learning. You must feel you have room to grow and learn, without constantly working at a pace guaranteed to lead to burnout. Your school needs you to be the lead learner; you need to model the idea that taking time for your own growth is important, just as it is for students and teachers.

How do you manage your own learning? How do you ensure that you are doing a good job? How do you try to ensure that you have not only the resources you need but also the learning opportunities? You can grow and move forward by participating in your own professional growth opportunities, whether through learning sessions or programs, online coursework, webinars, or other events held in your district, state, or beyond. You may opt to participate in National Association of Secondary School Principals (NASSP) or National Association of Elementary School Principals (NAESP), as well as the state affiliates of these organizations. Some organizations may have conferences or convenings that are general in nature or that focus on high-need topics. In North Carolina and in partnership with other organizations in other states and with the North Carolina Department of Public Instruction, the Friday Institute and the North Carolina Principal and Assistant Principal Association (NCPAPA) offer ongoing, job-embedded professional learning over the course of a year. Principals work in a cohort and spend five face-to-face days together with online community building and work in schools in between the sessions. The Friday Institute, in partnership with the Organization for Educational Technology and Curriculum (OETC), hosts a two-and-a-half day institute, Leading Schools, designed for school leaders.[5]

During the institute, principals from across the country gather to work on a problem of practice that they are facing in their schools. Through a design-thinking process, principals are exposed to new ideas and establish a network of principals from around the country who are working to solve similar problems related to personalized and digital learning.

Opportunities that are worth your time follow key aspects of professional learning: they are job-embedded, ongoing, and relevant to your context, and they provide you with opportunities to connect and collaborate with colleagues. These opportunities are directly focused on the transition to personalized and digital learning but also support the development of a community across the state, district, or region so that principals have others to connect with after the completion of the learning experience.

While some opportunities focus more on your looking inward, it is also critical that you look outward and build your own professional learning network. This group can help you when you have a question, allow you to share what you learn, provide a platform for reflection with questioning, and also cheer you on when things are going well. This group will help you sustain yourself when you hit roadblocks because many of the member principals have faced and sustained similar challenges. This group will push you to think differently and constantly share resources; it also can be a partner in new work. You can grow this network on your own, especially if you live in a more rural area or in a district that does not encourage collaboration across schools.

Talk with your district leaders about the resources you need and ask questions to see whether supports are available around technology or digital learning support, professional growth, and networking opportunities. The answers to these questions will help you understand the flexibility you have to make changes that are needed to accelerate progress toward your goals of personalized and digital learning. The answers will also help you understand the sustainability of your vision. Be sure that your sustainability plan is adaptable and built to last beyond one leader or one group of teachers.

TRY IT TOMORROW

1. **Take time to celebrate.** Celebrations are an important part of creating a positive school culture, but they can also play a role in retaining great teachers. Finding opportunities to celebrate your staff in sincere ways can go a long way in helping teachers feel good about the hard work they are putting in. Here are a couple of ideas on ways to celebrate your staff:

   - Place sticky notes with positive words of affirmation on the teachers' desks after you walk into their classrooms and see them doing something great.
   - Acknowledge staff members each week in your bulletin or e-mail update. Keep track of the teachers you have recognized so that you make sure you aren't pointing out a particular group of teachers too often while neglecting another group or individual. If you notice a teacher on your list that you haven't given a shout-out to, stop in to that teacher's classroom on several occasions looking for a positive piece of information that you can share with others.
   - Allow teachers to share praise or "good gossip" at the beginning of each staff meeting. This could also take the form of awards in which staff members recognize each other for something they have done that is deserving.

   Making celebrations a part of your culture will help your staff feel appreciated and will set a positive culture that can make a big difference in the way that teachers feel about their jobs.

9

Connect with Your Colleagues: Final Thoughts from Our Leaders

Learning from others who have implemented or are in the process of implementing personalized and digital learning environments is important. We can learn a lot from their success as well as their missteps. During the preparation for this book, we asked the principals involved, "What advice would you like to share with principals who are embarking on, ramping up, or continuing along this transition to personalized and digital learning?" You will not be surprised by their responses, but their words remind us of the core tenets of this book. This transition to personalized and digital learning is about the students and how we ensure that we understand and meet the needs of *each of our students*.

The principals highlighted throughout this book bring more than a century's worth of experience in leading schools. While we shared their examples and wisdom throughout, each leader provided two or three final pieces of advice for you, as fellow principals, as you begin or continue to lead your school and community in the transition to personalized and digital learning. We want to leave you with the voices of these master principals who have generously shared what they have learned and what has worked for them. You'll notice the following trends emerge in these parting remarks:

- Stay focused on student learning and outcomes.
- Don't forget your own learning.
- Engage stakeholders—you are not alone!
- Identify and trust excellent people as part of your team.

MICHAEL ARMSTRONG

1. *Ensure vision is focused on students with digital learning as a strategy.* Focus on the shared vision and use digital learning as a strategy to reach it. Digital learning itself is not an appropriate goal. The whole mindset is vision first. Don't try to keep up with the Joneses. Everything we did with digital learning at Bugg was about our vision of creating college pathways for students. Everything. That was something the community could get excited about.

2. *Empower.* [Focus] on empowerment—empowerment of teachers, kids, and parents. I was so eager to bring about change that I wanted to be a part of everything. You have to realize that you don't have to be a part of everything. You need to align to vision and let it go. This is a very technical thing. When I started as a principal at Bugg, I met with every staff person for forty-five minutes and asked them, "What do you love? What do you want to see changed? What advice do you have?" For three years, I lived by that list. That forty-five-minute investment created relationships that could not have ever been created in any other way. People remembered and wanted that of their new leader. Principals need to focus on one-on-one conversations and see what people get excited about.

JOHN BERNIA

1. *Start with yourself.* Take ownership of your learning and model your thinking.

2. *Trust your people.* Being the principal is about support and coaching, which requires a lot of listening. The best ideas come from classrooms. Give teachers the time and space to work together.

3. *Do not stray from the focus on student learning.* It's important to be flexible, but you must be rigid on growth and learning for *every* student, regardless of academic level or ability. Pay attention to your data and never stop asking about how much growth *every* learner is making.

ERIN FREW

1. *Be patient.* Change takes time. You have to be patient. Patience is really important. You need to be strategic and think very carefully about how to leverage your resources. And this can be really hard.

2. *Focus on student learning, not on grants.* Don't use money as the reason not to do something or to do something. It's a trap that I fell into—see a grant and see money. I spent the time writing the grant, but the money came with strings that may not have aligned with what I was doing. You do need resources, but not all are the same, particularly with technology and professional learning. I've gotten better at asking, "What do I want my students to be able to do, learn, know, and what experiences do I want them to have?"

ALISON HRAMIEC

1. *Pilot new ideas.* Pilot new ideas and ensure [the] staff and students' voice is incorporated in instructional decisions. What has worked well at BDEA is to be strategic about how we make change. New ideas are vetted at our instructional leadership team (ILT). Here we ask the questions. How does this change support or advance student learning? Does it make our work more or less sustainable? Once an idea is approved, we then pilot it with a small cluster of teachers and students. For example, one year we participated in a state-funded initiative that provides resources, professional development, and time for teachers to develop and pilot their own online courses with their students in their face-to-face classrooms. As we implemented this pilot over a series of years, I visited classrooms and talked with teachers and students about their learning experience. We made adjustments and tried out different versions of tech-enhanced teaching. At the end of three years, we realized two things: our high school student population was not engaged with this methodology, and teachers were not seeing tech-enhanced teaching as a time-saver. Instead, it was adding more to their workload with no academic gains in student learning. I realized through this process that as a trauma-sensitive competency-based school, we were already providing the personalized learning that technology was intended to support. As a school, we have systems and structures that make learning transparent to students, and students can move at their own pace. After this pilot period, our instructional leadership team instead saw the need to use technology to develop a comprehensive data collection system that provides students access to their academic

progress while also providing us the capacity to look at a variety of data points to measure student and whole school outcomes.

2. *Pay attention and personalize.* I find leading a school quite similar to teaching a classroom of students. It is important to pay attention to the students pushing back, to ask them questions and identify why they are resistant. For some, it is an easy fix; for others, the vision or path we are on needs to be fine-tuned. I have learned how to make decisions and move the school at a pace that is the speed of the collective voice. I see the strengths of each individual and also know where others struggle. I identify strategies to meet each staff where they are in their professional growth so that we as a school are a collaborative, supportive, and vibrant professional learning community. Meet staff where they are in their professional growth. Not top down; get with the program. This seems like an exploration, a learning process. *Move at the speed of the collective voice.*

3. *Say no.* Be willing to say no if what we've just spent years working on doesn't really serve us. There is no one-size-fits-all solution. Tech-enhanced learning is a tool—one of many—and it doesn't have to always be used in the same way.

SUZANNE LACEY

1. *Do your homework.* Research districts and schools who are already doing this well. Go and see, ask questions, and bring your core team/people with you. You need to establish that core team to identify and promote the vision. At our district, we started at Winterboro, and that became the model. Sometimes you have to start out small, but we moved fast. I worried about that, but as the process evolved, I became more comfortable with that. Even to this day, we still go back to Winterboro for defining moments.

2. *Work collaboratively and build a team.* Along the way, work collaboratively and build confidence among people working closely together. It's not the vision of one, but the vision of the collective work. You need to have a lot of honest conversations. There is no harm in that at all; it's just healthy. We may not all agree, but we come to consensus because the overarching goal is about students and what we can do to enhance opportunities for kids. Then it becomes okay if we disagree because

it goes back to what we can do for kids and how we can give them the best preparation to go into the world to do what they want to do.

TIM LAUER

1. *Engage in social media.* I find two aspects interesting when using social media. One aspect is that you can make connections and establish professional relationships with people doing similar work. You can know each other's work because of social media and you can connect with other like-minded or occupation-minded people. I find these professional connections to be very valuable. Another aspect of social media use is that it provides access to a vast number of experts. Whatever your topic, or interest, social media provides a way to connect with these individuals and to learn with and from them.

2. *Be active in your building.* Be in classrooms. Work to develop and learn systems that get you out of your office and in the rooms with the students and teachers. That's where the exciting stuff is happening. That's where technology comes into play. You need to break those chains of the office desk. Mobile technology allows us to work from any location in our school. You can just as easily answer a departmental e-mail from a third-grade classroom as from your office, and the third-grade classroom is way more interesting and exciting.

DEREK MCCOY

1. *See yourself as a lifelong learner.* Embrace—really embrace—that your learning is now lifelong and dynamic. It has to be as different as the learning we are designing for students. Next-generation leaders have to be PLN builders and connect with experts and other learners using digital tools to continue to grow their skills and understanding of what learning is and what teaching can/should look like. When we reap the benefit of this type of personalized learning, we can better build a vision for it for our students; we can better explain it and help others design it. I connect with and learn from experts daily. We have to be willing to be digital learners in order to understand what digital learning is.

2. Part of our jobs as school leaders today, no matter what our titles, is to think about our practices and beliefs, what we hold as dear and fundamental, and be willing to dig deep, shift slightly or clear the

table and start anew. This applies to many things in education, but it is very apparent when we talk about learning spaces. My advice to all school leaders, particularly to principals, is to keep learning about how the brain best learns, to keep trying to understand what motivates students and makes for engaging work. Then, take a critical look at the learning spaces in your school. If change needs to happen, sometimes it's just a matter of empowering teachers to take the reins. Sometimes your students can come up with innovative ideas about how to create spaces that they want to learn in every day. But ultimately, principals who dive into their PLNs will see the examples and rationales and methods others have used successfully to bring about great changes in their learning spaces, creating learning spaces that inspire students to achieve and learn at higher levels.

TROY MOORE

1. *Research well.* Take any opportunity to go and see what schools that have been successful in personalization are doing. Take early adopters with you whenever possible. Spend time with your early adopters and give them whatever they need to be successful. Get in the class and work with them. When they are ready to showcase, utilize their rooms as site labs.
2. *Trust your teachers to the extent possible.* Work toward providing a true safe and risk-taking environment. Do not be a micromanager. Show them it is okay to fail. We want them making sure that the students know it is okay to learn through failure and healthy struggle, and the teachers should be no different.
3. *Surround yourself with others who are passionate about this work.* That may be district-level support, fellow principals, high-level teachers in other schools, or PLN colleagues on Twitter. Caution: don't get into the comparison game because it will eat you alive. Be a good steward of your school. What are they ready for right now? What will they be ready for in a year?

AMY RICKARD

1. *Communicate.* The first thing is, *change is a process.* The communication piece is so important. For buy-in, you must be transparent. The

thing that can sabotage you is when people—teachers, parents, and students—don't feel like they are part of the process.

2. *Focus on student learning.* You have to keep the focus on student learning. You need to show how an effort helps student learning. Teachers have to see how this helps meet the standards by keeping students engaged and meeting the challenge. That is walking the talk. If it's not helping student learning, then you don't need to do it. If it is just for technology's sake, they don't need to do it. It is also important to understand age-appropriate instruction. In an elementary school, you have to understand the full range of grade levels. There is a big difference between kindergarten and fifth grade.

3. *Distribute leadership.* You can't do this yourself. You need to find a few champions and let them brainstorm possibilities. You need people who will criticize you and bring out challenges.

4. *Reflect on how you spend your time.* This is such a complete journey of reflection. Try to be reflective about what you should spend your time on and what's important. I see new principals spending time on things that aren't important, instead of leading. Part of this is just learning process and organization.

As you begin or continue this journey toward personalized and digital learning, we hope you will get to focus on many aspects of education that are core to why you entered the field in the first place. At times, you will feel as if you are going two steps forward and one step back, and you will have wonderful moments when you cannot believe what your students have created or accomplished. Keep the focus on the students—on what they need to be prepared for college, career, and citizenship. Build a culture that embodies trust of teachers, parents, and students. Never has this been more important than now.

The elements that we described in each of the chapters will help you build a school and culture that is ready for this transition, and they really all work together:

1. Create a vision focused on teaching and learning.
2. Engage stakeholders from the beginning, but don't stop there!
3. Employ change management and distributed leadership.
4. Build a culture of trust in which it is acceptable to fail.
5. Develop professional learning that is personalized and job-embedded.

6. Empower students with the Four Cs.
7. Create systems and structures that are sustainable and adaptable.
8. Build human capacity with teams.

As you tackle each of these areas, remember the three elements of leadership that are emphasized and more pronounced in the transition to personalized and digital learning:

- Model.
- Adapt to the pace of change.
- Articulate a shared vision.

Good leadership today is very much like good leadership of a decade or two ago, but these aspects are different or emphasized more strongly today than even five or ten years ago. Find your people and build your professional learning network through *#LeadingPDL*, by connecting with principals in your district or state, or by reaching out to those who seem to be further along on this journey or maybe just beginning. You definitely have one of the most challenging jobs in the world, but you do not need to be alone in this adventure.

TRY IT TOMORROW

1. **Connect with a partner.** Find someone to share ideas, successes, and failures with. These partnership are empowering, and they will make you a stronger leader.

2. **Connect with the principals highlighted in this book on social media.** Follow them to learn about what they're doing in their schools, what they're thinking about, and what they're excited about. Encourage other leaders in your professional learning network to do the same.

3. **Keep on keeping on.** Moving your school toward personalized and digital learning is a journey. Understand that there will be great days and difficult days. When you're struggling, reach out to someone who can reassure you that you're on the right path or help you correct your course. When you're succeeding, share those successes with others.

Notes

Introduction

1. James Zull, "The Art of Changing the Brain," *New Horizons for Learning*, http://www .education.jhu.edu/PD/newhorizons/Neurosciences/articles/The%20Art%20of%20 the%20Changing%20Brain/.
2. The Right Question Institute, "Percentage of Children Asking Questions," http:// rightquestion.org/percentage-children-asking-questions/.
3. Thomas L. Friedman, "Can't We Do Better?," *New York Times*, December 7, 2013, http://www.nytimes.com/2013/12/08/opinion/sunday/friedman-cant-we-do-better. html.
4. Department of Education Office of Technology, *National Education Technology Plan Update*, January 2017, 9, https://tech.ed.gov/files/2017/01/NETP17.pdf.
5. Mary Ann Wolf, *Innovate to Educate: Education System [Re]Design for Personalized Learning* (Washington, DC: ASCD, CCSSO, & SIIA, 2010), 14, http://www.ccsso.org /Documents/2010%20Symposium%20on%20Personalized%20Learning.pdf.
6. Friday Institute for Educational Innovation for the North Carolina State Board of Education-Department of Public Instruction, *North Carolina Digital Learning Plan*, September 2015, http://ncdlplan.fincsu.wpengine.com/wp-content/uploads/sites /10/2015/09/NCDLP_Summary8.31.15.pdf
7. Karen Seashore Louis et al., *Investigating the Link to Improved Student Learning*, 2010, http://www.wallacefoundation.org/knowledge-center/Documents/Investigating-the -Links-to-Improved-Student-Learning.pdf.
8. Michael Fullan, *The Principal: Three Keys to Maximizing Impact* (San Francisco: Jossey-Bass, 2014).

Chapter 1

1. Kristen Vogt, "How Next Gen Learning Can Support Student Agency," *Next Generation Learning Challenges*, January 14, 2016, http://nextgenlearning.org/blog/how-next -gen-learning-can-support-student-agency; citing Roland S. Barth, "The Leader as Learner," *Education Week*, 16, no. 23 (1997): 56.
2. Kim Carter, "The Good Learner" (presentation, The Friday Institute, North Carolina State University, May 10, 2016).
3. Wallace Foundation, *The School Principal as Leader: Guiding Schools to Better Teaching and Learning*, 2013, 7, http://www.wallacefoundation.org/knowledge-center /Documents/The-School-Principal-as-Leader-Guiding-Schools-to-Better-Teaching -and-Learning-2nd-Ed.pdf.
4. Mooresville Graded School District, *Mooresville Graded School District Strategic Plan 2013–2018*, http://mooresvillesd.finalsite.com/uploaded/documents/About_Us /Strategic_Plan_updated_with_retreat_work-1_copy.pdf?1396539189179.

5. Talledega County Schools website, http://www.tcboe.org/.

6. Mary Ann Wolf and Alex Dreier, *Making It Personal: Essential Elements of Hawk Ridge Elementary's Approach to Personalized Learning*, June 2015, http://www.fi.ncsu.edu/wp-content/uploads/2015/06/Hawk_Ridge_Elementary6.10.15.pdf.

7. Teach to One: Math, www.newclassrooms.org/how-it-works/daily-individualized-schedules/.

8. Liz Glowa and Jim Goodell, *Student-Centered Learning: Functional Requirements for Integrated Systems to Optimize Learning*, iNACOL, May 2016, 2, http://www.inacol.org/wp-content/uploads/2016/05/iNACOL_FunctionalRequirementsForIntegrated Systems.pdf.

9. Collaborative for Social and Emotional Learning (CASEL), http://www.casel.org/.

10. Clive Belfield et al., *The Economic Value of Social and Emotional Learning* (New York: Center for Benefit-Cost Studies in Education, 2015).

11. Joseph A. Durlak et al., "The Impact of Enhancing Student's Social and Emotional Learning: A Meta-Analysis of School-Based Universal Interventions," *Child Development*, 82 (Jan–Feb. 2011): 1.

12. Tom Vander Ark, "10 Tips for Developing Student Agency," *Education Week*, December 21, 2015, http://blogs.edweek.org/edweek/on_innovation/2015/12/10_tips_for_developing_student_agency.html.

13. C. A. Farrington, M. Roderick, E. Allensworth, J. Nagaoka, T. Seneca Keyes, D. W. Johnson, and N. O. Beechum, *Teaching Adolescents to Become Learners: The Role of Noncognitive Factors in Shaping School Performance* (Chicago, IL: University of Chicago Consortium on Chicago School Research), http://ccsr.uchicago.edu/publications/teaching-adolescents-become-learners-rolenoncognitive-factors-shaping-school; as quoted in Cheri Fancsali, Reva Jaffe-Walter, and Laurence Dessein, *Student Agency Practices in the Middle Shift Learning Networks*, IMPAQ International, Raikes Foundation, 2013, https://www.impaqint.com/sites/default/files/files/Student%20Agency%20Practices%20in%20the%20Middle%20Shift%20Learning%20Networks_0.pdf.

14. Fancsali, Jaffe-Walter, and Dessein, *Student Agency Practices in the Middle Shift Learning Networks*.

15. The Partnership for 21st Century Skills, www.p21.org; EdLeader21, www.edleader21.com.

16. Hewlett Foundation, www.hewlett.org.

Chapter 2

1. Michael Fullan, *The Principal: Three Keys for Maximizing Impact* (San Francisco: Jossy-Bass, 2014).

2. Mooresville Graded School District, http://www.mgsd.k12.nc.us/page.cfm?p=2783.

3. Jill Abbot et al., Technology-Enabled Personalized Learning Findings & Recommendations to Accelerate Implementation (Raleigh: NCSU Friday Institute, 2014), http://www.fi.ncsu.edu/wp-content/uploads/2014/02/TEPLS_report-FINAL-051415.pdf.

4. Stephen R. Covey, *The Seven Habits of Highly Effective People: Powerful Lessons in Personal Change* (New York: Free Press, 2004), 239.

5. The Experience Business, "Ten Top Tips for Great Focus Groups," 2012, http://www.theexperiencebusiness.co.uk/downloads/content-docs/top_ten_tips.pdf.

6. Common Sense Media, https://www.commonsensemedia.org/.

Chapter 3

1. W. Edwards Deming, "Rare Full-Length Interview," YouTube video, 56:26, February 1984, Posted by PQ Systems, March 28, 2016, https://www.youtube.com/watch?v=0yG hR1ybmN8&feature=youtu.be.
2. MetLife, "MetLife Survey of the American Teacher: Challenges for School Leadership, NY," 2012, www.metlife.com/teachersurvey.

Chapter 4

1. Richard Dufour, Rebecca Dufour, and Robert Eaker, Revisiting Professional Learning Communities at Work: New Insights for Improving Schools (Bloomington: Solution Tree Press, 2008).
2. Terrence Deal and Kent Peterson, "Strategies for Building School Cultures: Principals as Symbolic Leaders," in *Educational Leadership and School Culture*, ed. M. Sashkin and H. J. Walberg (Berkeley, CA: McCutchan, 1993), 89–99.
3. Talladega County Schools, "Digital Learning Day 2014: Talladega County Schools," YouTube video, 5:40, posted by Alliance for Excellent Education, February 7, 2014, https://www.youtube.com/watch?v=115tlF_jJBE.
4. GooseChase, https://www.goosechase.com/.
5. Marianne Rogowski, "Scavenger Hunts = Engagement + Fun!" *Common Sense Media* (blog), October 24, 2016, https://www.commonsense.org/education/blog/scavenger -hunts-engagement-fun.
6. BreakoutEDU, http://www.breakoutedu.com/.

Chapter 5

1. Linda Darling-Hammond et al., *Professional Learning in the Learning Profession: A Status Report on Teacher Development in the United States and Abroad* (Stanford: National Staff Development Council and The School Redesign Network, 2009).
2. Mary Ann Wolf, *Culture Shift: Teaching in a Learner-Centered Environment Powered by Digital Learning* (New York: Carnegie Corporation, 2012), 17.
3. Mary Ann Wolf, "A Study of Time and Tasks Required to Complete Job Related Work" (PhD dissertation, University of Virginia, 2002).
4. Joellen Killion et al., *Learning Matters* (Oxford: Learning Forward, 2012), 7.
5. Wolf, *Culture Shift*, 17.
6. Edcamp Foundation, http://www.edcamp.org/.
7. Digital Promise, https://bloomboard.com/microcredential/provider/ac2f23c8-274d -449d-ac3f-6ad29e399737.
8. Cyberman, http://www.cybraryman.com/chats.html.

Chapter 6

1. The Australian Society for Evidence Based Teaching, "Hattie & His High Impact Strategies for Teachers," http://www.evidencebasedteaching.org.au/hattie-his-high -impact-strategies/.
2. Learner Sketch Tool, http://qedfoundation.org/learner-sketch-tool/.
3. Charles Fadel, Bernie Trilling, and Maya Bialik, "The Role of Metacognition in Learning and Achievement," *KQED News by Mindshift*, August 10, 2016, https://ww2.kqed.org /mindshift/2016/08/10/the-role-of-metacognition-in-learning-and-achievement/.

4. "Continuum of Voice: What It Means for the Learner," *Personalize Learning*, January 10, 2016, http://www.personalizelearning.com/search?q=continuum+of+voice; "Choice Is More Than a Menu of Options," *Personalize Learning*, November 8, 2015, http://www.personalizelearning.com/search?q=continuum+of+choice; "Continuum of Engagement: Conversations That Engaged Twitter," *Personalize Learning*, April 19, 2016, http://www.personalizelearning.com/search?q=continuum+of+engagement.
5. "Flexible Classrooms: Providing the Learning Environment That Kids Need," YouTube video, 4:18, posted by Edutopia, August 3, 2015, https://www.youtube.com/watch?v=4cscJcRKYxA.

Chapter 7

1. "The Mooresville Graded School District in North Carolina reported a 64% reduction in disciplinary suspensions since the implementation of Digital Conversion, a 1:1 laptop programme; they also noted a 21% composite gain on state end-of-course tests during the same period (Mooresville Graded School District, 2011). In an efficacy study, Rockdale ISD in Texas found that students in the mobile learning programme were more engaged and discipline referrals related to policing student mobile phone use had decreased (L. Schad, personal communication, 26 October 2011)." Many of the schools led by principals featured in the book have shown improvement in student outcomes. Jennifer Fritschi and Mary Ann Wolf, *Turning on Mobile Learning in America* (Paris: UNESCO, 2012), 26.
2. Christine Fox and Rachel Jones, *The Broadband Imperative II: Equitable Access for Learning* (Washington, DC: State Educational Technology Directors Association, 2016), 2, http://www.setda.org/wp-content/uploads/2016/09/SETDA-Broadband-ImperativeII-Full-Document-Sept-8-2016.pdf.
3. SpeakUp, http://www.tomorrow.org/speakup/.
4. CAST, http://www.cast.org/our-work/about-udl.html#.WPPMWlPyvow.
5. Robin L. Flanigan, "Choosing the Right Digital Learning Device," *Education Week*, June 10, 2015, http://www.edweek.org/ew/articles/2015/06/11/choosing-the-right-digital-learning-device.html.
6. *BCES Revolutionizing Education* (blog), https://plus.google.com/communities/114214013588093224062.
7. Society for Learning Analytics Research, https://solaresearch.org/events/flare/ou2012/.
8. Mary Ann Wolf, *Capacity Enablers and Barriers for Learning Analytics: Implications for Policy and Practice* (Washington, DC: Alliance for Excellent Education, 2014), 2, http://all4ed.org/reports-factsheets/capacity-enablers-and-barriers-for-learning-analytics-implications-for-policy-and-practice/.
9. Ibid., 7.
10. Geraldine O'Neil, *UCD Assessment Redesign Project: The Balance Between Assessment FOR and OF Learning*, October 15, 2012, https://www.ucd.ie/t4cms/UCDTLA0044.pdf.
11. Project Tomorrow, http://www.tomorrow.org/speakup/2016-digital-learning-reports-from-blackboard-and-speak-up.html.
12. Christopher Piehler, "Survey Reveals Students' Mobile Device Preferences," *The Journal*, September 21, 2015, https://thejournal.com/articles/2015/09/21/survey-reveals-students-mobile-device-preferences.aspx.
13. Common Sense Media, https://www.commonsense.org/education/digital-citizenship.

14. KidSmartz, http://www.kidsmartz.org/.

15. Consortium for School Networking, "SmartIT: Total Cost of Ownership Assessment," 2016, http://www.cosn.org/tco.

16. ERStrategies, https://www.erstrategies.org/hold-em.

17. ERStrategies, https://www.erstrategies.org/info/tools.

Chapter 8

1. Alexandria Neason, "Half of Teachers Leave the Job After Five Years. Here's What to Do About It," *The Hechinger Report*, July 18, 2014.

2. Harris Interactive, *The MetLife Survey of the American Teacher*, February 2013, https://www.metlife.com/assets/cao/foundation/MetLife-Teacher-Survey-2012.pdf, 50.

3. Opportunity Culture, http://opportunityculture.org/.

4. Eric Westervelt, "What Are the Main Reasons Teachers Call It Quits?," NPR, October 24, 2016, http://www.npr.org/sections/ed/2016/10/24/495186021/what-are-the-main-reasons-teachers-call-it-quits).

5. OETC, http://events.oetc.org/.

Acknowledgments

Thank you to our nine personalized learning leaders featured in this book:

Michael Armstrong
John Bernia
Erin Frew
Alison Hramiec
Suzanne Lacey
Tim Lauer
Derek McCoy
Troy Moore
Amy Rickard

Thanks also to the following:

John Mayher
Tom Williams
Barbara Treacy
Glenn Kleiman
Kathy Spencer
Frances Bradburn
Sara Hall
Rachel Jones
Elsie Brumback
The Team at the Friday Institute

Our colleagues and mentors throughout North Carolina and in Wake County Public Schools, the Alliance for Excellent Education, and State Educational Technology Directors Association (SETDA) throughout the years who have pushed our thinking and have given us opportunities to learn, try new things, and grow.

The amazing educators we have worked with and continue to work with on a daily basis: your passion and drive inspire us and reassure us that the future is bright for the students you serve.

And the students who remind us of our *why* everyday!

From Mary Ann Wolf:

To my Mom for making education, teaching, and personalized learning part of who I am.

To Brian for always believing in me, and to Marin, Matthew, and Andrew for being curious about learning, for helping me see what is possible, and for being the world's greatest cheerleaders.

From Elizabeth Bobst:

For Katie, Jack, and Matt for showing me that there is beauty and value in individual differences.

From Nancy Mangum:

To my parents for being wonderful role models and teaching me to serve others through my words and actions. And to Brandon, my friends, and family for believing in me and encouraging me to pursue my dreams.

About the Authors

Mary Ann Wolf is the Director of Digital Learning Programs at the Friday Institute for Educational Innovation at North Carolina State University. She began her career in education as a fifth-grade teacher and has worked with national, state, district, and school leaders across the country in building capacity for personalized and digital learning. She and her team lead ongoing, job-embedded professional learning to guide superintendents, district teams, and principals, coaches, and teachers. Mary Ann played a lead role in developing and facilitating the Digital Learning Transition MOOC-Ed and the Learning Differences MOOC-Ed. She has written extensively on culture, personalized learning, and digital learning, including *Innovate to Educate: Education System [Re]Design for Personalized Learning*, an influential report based on a symposium held by SIIA, ASCD, and CCSSO. She also coauthored *Culture Shift: Teaching in a Learner-Centered Environment Powered by Digital Learning* for the Alliance for Excellent Education and two reports on mobile learning in North America for UNESCO and CoSN. She was previously the executive director of the State Educational Technology Directors Association (SETDA) and spent many years in the nation's capital advocating for the importance of personalized and digital learning to meet the needs of each student. Mary Ann was a member of the NAEP Technology Literacy Assessment steering committee. She also testified before the US House of Representatives Education and Labor Committee; SETDA hosted, with the National Science Foundation, Future of Learning educational technology showcases for members of Congress and staffers in the House and Senate. Connect with Mary Ann on Twitter at @maryannwolfed or by e-mail at wolfed.maryann@gmail.com.

Elizabeth Bobst is a writer, editor, and educator focusing on ESOL and international education. She began her teaching career as a middle/high school English teacher and volleyball coach and has taught in classrooms up and down the east coast. After earning her TESOL certification from NCSU in 2013,

Elizabeth now works with adults learning English as a second language and who are using English as a tool to improve their lives. Interested in sharing culture as well as language, Elizabeth has taught in several different countries. Her writing focuses on personalized and digital learning, as well as equity issues in education. Connect with Elizabeth on her website elizabethbobst.com.

Nancy Mangum is the Digital Learning Lead at The Friday Institute for Educational Innovation at North Carolina State University. Nancy is passionate about helping educators create learning environments that empower all students and ignite their passion for learning and teaching. She has developed several comprehensive programs for school leaders including the Leadership in Blended and Digital Learning program that is being run in sixteen organizations and states around the country. Her work at the institute also includes guiding principals and district leaders as they implement digital transitions through leadership development, strategic planning, and coaching.

She leads several projects at the Friday Institute including the Digital Leaders Coaching Network, the Leadership in Blended and Digital Learning Program, and Leading Schools Project. Nancy is a contributor to the National Future Ready Summits sponsored by the US Department of Education and is a content developer and summit facilitator for the Alliance for Excellent Education. She has also been the president of NCTIES. She brings a depth of knowledge about curriculum, pedagogy, and instructional technology, with past experiences as a classroom teacher, technology facilitator, and district leader. Connect with Nancy on Twitter at @nmangum or via e-mail at nkmangum@gmail.com.

Index